P9-CND-152

Wherever You Go,
There You Are

Wherever You Go, There You Are

✧

Mindfulness Meditation in Everyday Life

✧

Jon Kabat-Zinn

HYPERION

NEW YORK

Reprint permissions appear on page 279

Library of Congress Cataloging-in-Publication Data
Kabat-Zinn, Jon.
Wherever you go, there you are: mindfulness meditation
in everyday life /Jon Kabat-Zinn.—1st ed.
p. cm
ISBN 0-7868-8070-8
I. Meditation. 2. Attention. I. Title.
II. Title: Mindfulness meditation in everyday life.
BF637.m4K23   1994
155.9'042—dc20   93-24038   CIP

10th Anniversary Edition ISBN: 1-4013-0778-7

Hyperion books are available for special promotions and premiums.
For details contact Michael Rentas, Manager, Inventory and Premium
Sales, Hyperion, 77 West 66th Street, 11th floor, New York, New York
10023, or call 212-456-0133.

6   7   8   9   10

For Myla, Will, Naushon, and Serena,
wherever you go

I would like to thank Myla Kabat-Zinn, Sarah Doering, Larry Rosenberg, John Miller, Danielle Levi Alvares, Randy Paulsen, Martin Diskin, Dennis Humphrey, and Ferris Urbanowski for reading early drafts of the manuscript and giving me their valuable insights and encouragement. My deep appreciation to Trudy and Barry Silverstein for the use of Rocky Horse Ranch during an intensive period of early writing, and to Jason and Wendy Cook for Western adventures during those wonderful days. Profound gratitude to my editors, Bob Miller and Mary Ann Naples, for their deep commitment to excellence and the pleasure of working with them. I thank them, the Hyperion family, literary agent, Patricia Van der Leun, Dorothy Schmiderer Baker, book designer, and Beth Maynard, artist, for the care and attention they gave to the birthing of this book.

Coming to Our Senses: Healing Ourselves and the World Through Mindfulness

Everyday Blessings: The Inner Work of Mindful Parenting (with Myla Kabat-Zinn)

Full Catastrophe Living: Using the Wisdom of Your Body and Mind to Face Stress, Pain, and Illness

Contents

Introduction

Guess what? When it comes right down to it, wherever you go, there you are. Whatever you wind up doing, that's what you've wound up doing. Whatever you are thinking right now, *that's* what's on your mind. Whatever has happened to you, it has already happened. The important question is, how are you going to handle it? In other words, "Now what?"

Like it or not, this moment is all we really have to work with. Yet we all too easily conduct our lives as if forgetting momentarily that we are *here*, where we already are, and that we are *in* what we are already in. In every moment, we find ourselves at the crossroad of here and now. But when the cloud of forgetfulness over where we are now sets in, in that very moment we get lost. "Now what?" becomes a real problem.

By lost, I mean that we momentarily lose touch with ourselves and with the full extent of our possibilities. Instead, we fall into a robotlike way of seeing and thinking and doing. In those moments, we break contact with what is deepest in ourselves and affords us perhaps our greatest opportunities for creativity, learning, and growing. If we are not careful, those clouded moments can stretch out and become most of our lives.

To allow ourselves to be truly in touch with where we already are, no matter where that is, we have got to pause in our experience long enough to let the present moment sink in; long enough to actually *feel* the present moment, to see it in its fullness, to hold it in awareness and thereby come to know and understand it better. Only then can we accept the truth of this moment of our life, learn from it, and move on. Instead, it often seems as if we are preoccupied with the past, with what has already happened, or with a future that hasn't arrived yet. We look for someplace else to stand, where we hope things will be better, happier, more the way we want them to be, or the way they used to be. Most of the time we are only partially aware of this inner tension, if we are aware of it at all. What is more, we are also only partially aware at best of exactly what we are doing in and with our lives, and the effects our actions and, more subtly, our thoughts have on what we see and don't see, what we do and don't do.

For instance, we usually fall, quite unawares, into assuming that what we are thinking—the ideas and opinions that we harbor at any given time—are "the truth" about what is "out there" in the world and "in here" in our minds. Most of the time, it just isn't so.

We pay a high price for this mistaken and unexamined assumption, for our almost willful ignoring of the richness of our present moments. The fallout accumulates silently, coloring our lives without our knowing it or being able to do something about it. We may never quite be where we actually are, never quite touch the fullness of our possibilities. Instead, we lock ourselves into a personal fiction that we already know who we are, that we know where we are and where we are going, that we know what is happening—all the while remaining enshrouded in thoughts, fantasies, and impulses, mostly about the past and about the future, about what we want and like, and what we fear and don't like, which spin out continuously, veiling our direction and the very ground we are standing on.

The book you have in your hands is about waking up from such dreams and from the nightmares they often turn into. Not knowing that you are even in such a dream is what the Buddhists call "ignorance," or mindlessness. Being in touch with this not knowing is called "mindfulness." The work of waking up from these dreams is the work of meditation, the systematic cultivation of wakefulness, of present-moment awareness. This waking up goes hand in hand with what we might call "wisdom," a seeing more deeply into cause and effect and the interconnectedness of things, so that we are no longer caught in a dream-dictated reality of our own creation. To find our way, we will need to pay more attention to this moment. It is the only time that we have in which to live, grow, feel, and change. We will need to become more aware of and take precautions against the incredible pull of the Scylla and Charybdis of past and future, and the dreamworld they offer us in place of our lives.

When we speak of meditation, it is important for you to know that this is not some weird cryptic activity, as our popular culture might have it. It does not involve becoming some kind of zombie, vegetable, self-absorbed narcissist, navel gazer, "space cadet," cultist, devotee, mystic, or Eastern philosopher. Meditation is simply about being yourself and knowing something about who that is. It is about coming to realize that you are on a path whether you like it or not, namely, the path that is your life. Meditation may help us see that this path we call our life has direction; that it is always unfolding, moment by moment; and that what happens now, in this moment, influences what happens next.

If what happens now does influence what happens next, then doesn't it makes sense to look around a bit from time to time so that you are more in touch with what is happening now, so that you can take your inner and outer bearings and perceive with clarity the path that you are actually on and the direction in which you are going? If you do so, maybe you will be in a better position to chart a course for yourself that is truer to your inner being—a soul path, a path with heart, *your* path with a capital P. If not, the sheer momentum of your unconsciousness in this moment just colors the next moment. The days, months, and years quickly go by unnoticed, unused, unappreciated.

It is all too easy to remain on something of a fog-enshrouded, slippery slope right into our graves; or, in the fog-dispelling clarity which on occasion precedes the moment of death, to wake up and realize that what we had thought all those years about how life was to be lived and what was important were at best unexamined half-truths based on fear or ignorance, only our own life-limiting ideas, and not the truth or the way our life had to be at all.

No one else can do this job of waking up for us, although our family and friends do sometimes try desperately to get through to us, to help us see more clearly or break out of our own blindnesses. But waking up is ultimately something that each one of us can only do for ourselves. When it comes down to it, wherever *you* go, there *you* are. It's *your* life that is unfolding.

At the end of a long life dedicated to teaching mindfulness, the Buddha, who probably had his share of followers who were hoping he might make it easier for them to find their own paths, summed it up for his disciples this way: "Be a light unto yourself."

In my previous book, *Full Catastrophe Living*, I tried to make the path of mindfulness accessible to mainstream Americans so that it would not feel Buddhist or mystical so much as sensible. Mindfulness has to do above all with attention and awareness, which are universal human qualities. But in our society, we tend to take these capacities for granted and don't think to develop them systematically in the service of self-understanding and wisdom. Meditation is the process by which we go about deepening our attention and awareness, refining them, and putting them to greater practical use in our lives.

Full Catastrophe Living can be thought of as a navigational chart, intended for people facing physical or emotional pain or reeling from the effects of too much stress. The aim was to challenge the reader to realize, through his or her direct experiences of paying attention to things we all so often ignore, that there might be very real reasons for integrating mindfulness into the fabric of one's life.

Not that I was suggesting that mindfulness is some kind of a cureall or dimestore solution to life's problems. Far from it. I don't know of any magical solutions and, frankly, I am not looking for one. A full life is painted with broad brush strokes. Many paths can lead to understanding and wisdom. Each of us has different needs to address and things worth pursuing over the course of a lifetime. Each of us has to chart our own course, and it has to fit what we are ready for.

You certainly have to be ready for meditation. You have to come to it at the right time in your life, at a point where you are ready to listen carefully to your own voice, to your own heart, to your own breathing—to just be present for them and with them, without having to go anywhere or make anything better or different. This is hard work.

I wrote *Full Catastrophe Living* thinking of the people referred to us as patients in our stress reduction clinic at the University of Massachusetts Medical Center. I was moved to do so by the remarkable transformations in mind and body that many people report as they put aside trying to change the severe problems that brought them to the clinic in the first place, and engage over an eight-week period in the intensive discipline of opening and listening that characterizes the practice of mindfulness.

As a navigational chart, *Full Catastrophe Living* had to supply enough detail so that someone in significant need could plot his or her own course with care. It had to speak to the pressing needs of people with serious medical problems and chronic pain, as well as to those suffering in different kinds of stressful situations. For these reasons, it had to include a good deal of information on stress and illness, health and healing, as well as extensive instructions on how to meditate.

This book is different. It is meant to provide brief and easy access to the essence of mindfulness meditation and its applications, for people whose lives may or may not be dominated by immediate problems of stress, pain, and illness. It is offered particularly for those who resist structured programs and for people who don't like to be told what to do but are curious enough about mindfulness and its relevance to try to piece things together for themselves with a few hints and suggestions here and there.

At the same time, this book is also offered to those who are already practicing meditation and wish to expand, deepen, and reinforce their commitment to a life of greater awareness and insight. Here, in brief chapters, the focus is on the spirit of mindfulness, both in our formal attempts at practice and in our efforts to bring it into all aspects of our daily lives. Each chapter is a glimpse through one face of the multifaceted diamond of mindfulness. The chapters are related to each other by tiny rotations of the crystal. Some may sound similar to others, but each facet is also different, unique.

This exploration of the diamond of mindfulness is offered for all those who would chart a course toward greater sanity and wisdom in their lives. What is required is a willingness to look deeply at one's present moments, no matter what they hold, in a spirit of generosity, kindness toward oneself, and openness toward what might be possible.

Part One explores the rationale and background for taking on or deepening a personal practice of mindfulness. It challenges the reader to experiment with introducing mindfulness into his or her life in a number of different ways. Part Two explores some basic aspects of formal meditation practice. Formal practice refers to specific periods of time in which we purposefully stop other activity and engage in particular methods of cultivating mindfulness and concentration. Part Three explores a range of applications and perspectives on mindfulness. Certain chapters in all three parts end with explicit suggestions for incorporating aspects of both formal and informal mindfulness practice into one's life. These are found under the heading "TRY."

This volume contains sufficient instructions to engage in meditation practice on one's own, without the use of other materials or supports. However, many people find it helpful to use audiotapes in the beginning to support the daily discipline of a formal meditation practice, and to guide them in the instructions until they get the hang of it and wish to practice on their own. Others find that even after years of practice, it is helpful on occasion to make use of tapes. To this end, a new series of mindfulness meditation practice tapes (Series 2) has been prepared in conjunction with this book. These tapes range in length from ten minutes to half an hour; they give the reader who is new to mindfulness practice a range of techniques to experiment with, as well as room to decide what length of formal practice is appropriate for a given time and place. The Series 2 tapes are listed in the order form at the back of this book, along with the 45-minute tapes from Series 1 which accompany *Full Catastrophe Living*.

Part One

The Bloom of the Present Moment

Only that day dawns to which we are awake.

HENRY DAVID THOREAU, *Walden*

What Is Mindfulness?

Mindfulness is an ancient Buddhist practice which has profound relevance for our present-day lives. This relevance has nothing to do with Buddhism per se or with becoming a Buddhist, but it has everything to do with waking up and living in harmony with oneself and with the world. It has to do with examining who we are, with questioning our view of the world and our place in it, and with cultivating some appreciation for the fullness of each moment we are alive. Most of all, it has to do with being in touch.

From the Buddhist perspective, our ordinary waking state of consciousness is seen as being severely limited and limiting, resembling in many respects an extended dream rather than wakefulness. Meditation helps us wake up from this sleep of automaticity and unconsciousness, thereby making it possible for us to live our lives with access to the full spectrum of our conscious and unconscious possibilities. Sages, yogis, and Zen masters have been exploring this territory systematically for thousands of years; in the process they have learned something which may now be profoundly beneficial in the West to counterbalance our cultural orientation toward controlling and subduing nature rather than honoring that we are an intimate part of it. Their collective experience suggests that by investigating inwardly our own nature as beings and, particularly, the nature of our own minds through careful and systematic self-observation, we may be able to live lives of greater satisfaction, harmony, and wisdom. It also offers a view of the world which is complementary to the predominantly reductionist and materialistic one currently dominating Western thought and institutions. But this view is neither particularly "Eastern" nor mystical. Thoreau saw the same problem with our ordinary mind state in New England in 1846 and wrote with great passion about its unfortunate consequences.

Mindfulness has been called the heart of Buddhist meditation. Fundamentally, mindfulness is a simple concept. Its power lies in its practice and its applications. Mindfulness means paying attention in a particular way: on purpose, in the present moment, and nonjudgmentally. This kind of attention nurtures greater awareness, clarity, and acceptance of present-moment reality. It wakes us up to the fact that our lives unfold only in moments. If we are not fully present for many of those moments, we may not only miss what is most valuable in our lives but also fail to realize the richness and the depth of our possibilities for growth and transformation.

A diminished awareness of the present moment inevitably creates other problems for us as well through our unconscious and automatic actions and behaviors, often driven by deepseated fears and insecurities. These problems tend to build over time if they are not attended to and can eventually leave us feeling stuck and out of touch. Over time, we may lose confidence in our ability to redirect our energies in ways that would lead to greater satisfaction and happiness, perhaps even to greater health.

Mindfulness provides a simple but powerful route for getting ourselves unstuck, back into touch with our own wisdom and vitality. It is a way to take charge of the direction and quality of our own lives, including our relationships within the family, our relationship to work and to the larger world and planet, and most fundamentally, our relationship with ourself as a person.

The key to this path, which lies at the root of Buddhism, Taoism, and yoga, and which we also find in the works of people like Emerson, Thoreau, and Whitman, and in Native American wisdom, is an appreciation for the present moment and the cultivation of an intimate relationship with it through a continual attending to it with care and discernment. It is the direct opposite of taking life for granted.

The habit of ignoring our present moments in favor of others yet to come leads directly to a pervasive lack of awareness of the web of life in which we are embedded. This includes a lack of awareness and understanding of our own mind and how it influences our perceptions and our actions. It severely limits our perspective on what it means to be a person and how we are connected to each other and to the world around us. Religion has traditionally been the domain of such fundamental inquiries within a spiritual framework, but mindfulness has little to do with religion, except in the most fundamental meaning of the word, as an attempt to appreciate the deep mystery of being alive and to acknowledge being vitally connected to all that exists.

When we commit ourselves to paying attention in an open way, without falling prey to our own likes and dislikes, opinions and prejudices, projections and expectations, new possibilities open up and we have a chance to free ourselves from the straitjacket of unconsciousness.

I like to think of mindfulness simply as the art of conscious living. You don't have to be a Buddhist or a yogi to practice it. In fact, if you know anything about Buddhism, you will know that the most important point is to be yourself and not try to become anything that you are not already. Buddhism is fundamentally about being in touch with your own deepest nature and letting it flow out of you unimpeded. It has to do with waking up and seeing things as they are. In fact, the word "Buddha" simply means one who has awakened to his or her own true nature.

So, mindfulness will not conflict with any beliefs or traditions—religious or for that matter scientific—nor is it trying to sell you anything, especially not a new belief system or ideology. It is simply a practical way to be more in touch with the fullness of your being through a systematic process of self-observation, self-inquiry, and mindful action. There is nothing cold, analytical, or unfeeling about it. The overall tenor of mindfulness practice is gentle, appreciative, and nurturing. Another way to think of it would be "heartfulness."

*

A student once said: "When I was a Buddhist, it drove my parents and friends crazy, but when I am a buddha, nobody is upset at all."

Simple but Not Easy

While it may be simple to practice mindfulness, it is not necessarily easy. Mindfulness requires effort and discipline for the simple reason that the forces that work against our being mindful, namely, our habitual unawareness and automaticity, are exceedingly tenacious. They are so strong and so much out of our consciousness that an inner commitment and a certain kind of work are necessary just to keep up our attempts to capture our moments in awareness and sustain mindfulness. But it is an intrinsically satisfying work because it puts us in touch with many aspects of our lives that are habitually overlooked and lost to us.

It is also enlightening and liberating work. It is enlightening in that it literally allows us to see more clearly, and therefore come to understand more deeply, areas in our lives that we were out of touch with or unwilling to look at. This may include encountering deep emotions—such as grief, sadness, woundedness, anger, and fear—that we might not ordinarily allow ourselves to hold in awareness or express consciously. Mindfulness can also help us to appreciate feelings such as joy, peacefulness, and happiness which often go by fleetingly and unacknowledged. It is liberating in that it leads to new ways of being in our own skin and in the world, which can free us from the ruts we so often fall into. It is empowering as well, because paying attention in this way opens channels to deep reservoirs of creativity, intelligence, imagination, clarity, determination, choice, and wisdom within us.

We tend to be particularly unaware that we are thinking virtually all the time. The incessant stream of thoughts flowing through our minds leaves us very little respite for inner quiet. And we leave precious little room for ourselves anyway just to be, without having to run around doing things all the time. Our actions are all too frequently driven rather than undertaken in awareness, driven by those perfectly ordinary thoughts and impulses that run through the mind like a coursing river, if not a waterfall. We get caught up in the torrent and it winds up submerging our lives as it carries us to places we may not wish to go and may not even realize we are headed for.

Meditation means learning how to get out of this current, sit by its bank and listen to it, learn from it, and then use its energies to guide us rather than to tyrannize us. This process doesn't magically happen by itself. It takes energy. We call the effort to cultivate our ability to be in the present moment "practice" or "meditation practice."

*

Question: How can I set right a tangle which is entirely below the level of my consciousness?

Nisargadatta: By being with yourself . . . by watching yourself in your daily life with alert interest, with the intention to understand rather than to judge, in full acceptance of whatever may emerge, because it is there, you encourage the deep to come to the surface and enrich your life and consciousness with its captive energies. This is the great work of awareness; it removes obstacles and releases energies by under-standing the nature of life and mind. Intelligence is the door to freedom and alert attention is the mother of intelligence.

NISARGADATTA MAHARAJ, *I Am That*

Stopping

People think of meditation as some kind of special activity, but this is not exactly correct. Meditation is simplicity itself. As a joke, we sometimes say: "Don't just do something, sit there." But meditation is not just about sitting, either. It is about stopping and being present, that is all. Mostly we run around doing. Are you able to come to a stop in your life, even for one moment? Could it be *this* moment? What would happen if you did?

A good way to stop all the doing is to shift into the "being mode" for a moment. Think of yourself as an eternal witness, as timeless. Just watch this moment, without trying to change it at all. What is happening? What do you feel? What do you see? What do you hear?

The funny thing about stopping is that as soon as you do it, here you are. Things get simpler. In some ways, it's as if you died and the world continued on. If you did die, all your responsibilities and obligations would immediately evaporate. Their residue would somehow get worked out without you. No one else can take over your unique agenda. It would die or peter out with you just as it has

11

for everyone else who has ever died. So you don't need to worry about it in any absolute way.

If this is true, maybe you don't need to make one more phone call right now, even if you think you do. Maybe you don't need to read something just now, or run one more errand. By taking a few moments to "die on purpose" to the rush of time while you are still living, you free yourself to have time for the present. By "dying" now in this way, you actually become more alive now. This is what stopping can do. There is nothing passive about it. And when you decide to go, it's a different kind of going because you stopped. The stopping actually makes the going more vivid, richer, more textured. It helps keep all the things we worry about and feel inadequate about in perspective. It gives us guidance.

TRY: Stopping, sitting down, and becoming aware of your breathing once in a while throughout the day. It can be for five minutes, or even five seconds. Let go into full acceptance of the present moment, including how you are feeling and what you perceive to be happening. For these moments, don't try to change anything at all, just breathe and let go. Breathe and let be. Die to having to have anything be different in this moment; in your mind and in your heart, give yourself permission to allow this moment to be exactly as it is, and allow yourself to be exactly as you are. Then, when you're ready, move in the direction your heart tells you to go, mindfully and with resolution.

This Is It

New Yorker cartoon: Two Zen monks in robes and shaved heads, one young, one old, sitting side by side cross-legged on the floor. The younger one is looking somewhat quizzically at the older one, who is turned toward him and saying: "Nothing happens next. This is it."

It's true. Ordinarily, when we undertake something, it is only natural to expect a desirable outcome for our efforts. We want to see results, even if it is only a pleasant feeling. The sole exception I can think of is meditation. Meditation is the only intentional, systematic human activity which at bottom is about *not* trying to improve yourself or get anywhere else, but simply to realize where you already are. Perhaps its value lies precisely in this. Maybe we all need to do one thing in our lives simply for its own sake.

But it would not quite be accurate to call meditation a "doing." It is more accurately described as a "being." When we understand that "This is it," it allows us to let go of the past and the future and wake up to what we are now, in this moment.

People usually don't get this right away. They want to meditate in order to relax, to experience a special state, to become a better person, to reduce some stress or pain, to break out of old habits and patterns, to become free or enlightened. All valid reasons to take up meditation practice, but all equally fraught with problems if you expect those things to happen just because now you are meditating. You'll get caught up in wanting to have a "special experience" or in looking for signs of progress, and if you don't feel something special pretty quickly, you may start to doubt the path you have chosen, or to wonder whether you are "doing it right."

In most domains of learning, this is only reasonable. Of course you have to see progress sooner or later to keep at something. But meditation is different. From the perspective of meditation, every state is a special state, every moment a special moment.

When we let go of wanting something else to happen in this moment, we are taking a profound step toward being able to encounter what is here now. If we hope to go anywhere or develop ourselves in any way, we can only step from where we are standing. If we don't really know where we are standing—a knowing that comes directly from the cultivation of mindfulness—we may only go in circles, for all our efforts and expectations. So, in meditation practice, the best way to get somewhere is to let go of trying to get anywhere at all.

✿

If your mind isn't clouded by unnecessary things,
This is the best season of your life.

W U - M E N

T R Y : Reminding yourself from time to time: "This is it." See if there is anything at all that it cannot be applied to. Remind yourself that acceptance of the present moment has nothing to do with resignation in the face of what is happening. It simply means a clear acknowledgment that *what is happening is happening*. Acceptance doesn't tell you what to do. What happens next, what you choose to do, that has to come out of your understanding of this moment. You might try acting out of a deep knowing of "This is it." Does it influence how you choose to proceed or respond? Is it possible for you to contemplate that in a very real way, *this* may actually be the best season, the best moment of your life? If that was so, what would it mean for you?

Capturing Your Moments

The best way to capture moments is to pay attention. This is how we cultivate mindfulness. Mindfulness means being awake. It means knowing what you are doing. But when we start to focus in on what our own mind is up to, for instance, it is not unusual to quickly go unconscious again, to fall back into an automatic-pilot mode of unawareness. These lapses in awareness are frequently caused by an eddy of dissatisfaction with what we are seeing or feeling in that moment, out of which springs a desire for something to be different, for things to change.

You can easily observe the mind's habit of escaping from the present moment for yourself. Just try to keep your attention focused on any object for even a short period of time. You will find that to cultivate mindfulness, you may have to remember over and over again to be awake and aware. We do this by reminding ourselves to look, to feel, to be. It's that simple . . . checking in from moment to moment, sustaining awareness across a stretch of timeless moments, being here, now.

TRY: Asking yourself in this moment, "Am I awake?," "Where is my mind right now?"

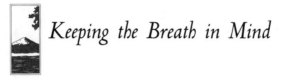

Keeping the Breath in Mind

It helps to have a focus for your attention, an anchor line to tether you to the present moment and to guide you back when the mind wanders. The breath serves this purpose exceedingly well. It can be a true ally. Bringing awareness to our breathing, we remind ourselves that we are here now, so we might as well be fully awake for whatever is already happening.

Our breathing can help us in capturing our moments. It's surprising that more people don't know about this. After all, the breath is always here, right under our noses. You would think just by chance we might have come across its usefulness at one point or another. We even have the phrase, "I didn't have a moment to breathe" (or "to catch my breath") to give us a hint that moments and breathing might be connected in an interesting way.

To use your breathing to nurture mindfulness, just tune in to the feeling of it . . . the feeling of the breath coming into your body and the feeling of the breath leaving your body. That's all. Just feeling the breath. Breathing and knowing that you're breathing. This doesn't mean deep breathing or forcing your breathing, or trying to feel something special, or wondering whether you're doing it right. It doesn't mean thinking about your breathing, either. It's just a bare bones awareness of the breath moving in and the breath moving out.

It doesn't have to be for a long time at any one stretch. Using the breath to bring us back to the present moment takes no time at all, only a shift in attention. But great adventures await you if you give yourself a little time to string moments of awareness together, breath by breath, moment to moment.

TRY: Staying with one full inbreath as it comes in, one full outbreath as it goes out, keeping your mind open and free for just this moment, just this breath. Abandon all ideas of getting somewhere or having anything happen. Just keep returning to the breath when the mind wanders, stringing moments of mindfulness together, breath by breath. Try it every once in a while as you read this book.

*

Kabir says: Student, tell me, what is God?
He is the breath inside the breath.

KABIR

Practice, Practice, Practice

It helps to keep at it. As you begin befriending your breath, you see immediately that unawareness is everywhere. Your breath teaches you that not only does unawareness go with the territory, it *is* the territory. It does this by showing you, over and over again, that it's not so easy to stay with the breath even if you want to. Lots of things intrude, carry us off, prevent us from concentrating. We see that the mind has gotten cluttered over the years, like an attic, with old bags and accumulated junk. Just knowing this is a big step in the right direction.

Practice Does Not Mean Rehearsal

We use the word "practice" to describe the cultivation of mindfulness, but it is not meant in the usual sense of a repetitive rehearsing to get better and better so that a performance or a competition will go as well as possible.

Mindfulness practice means that we commit fully in each moment to being present. There is no "performance." There is just this moment. We are not trying to improve or to get anywhere else. We are not even running after special insights or visions. Nor are we forcing ourselves to be non-judgmental, calm, or relaxed. And we are certainly not promoting self-consciousness or indulging in self-preoccupation. Rather, we are simply inviting ourselves to interface with this moment in full awareness, with the intention to embody as best we can an orientation of calmness, mindfulness, and equanimity right here and right now.

Of course, with continued practice and the right kind of firm yet gentle effort, calmness and mindfulness and equanimity develop and deepen on their own, out of your commitment to dwell in stillness and to observe without reacting and without judging. Realizations and insights, profound experiences of stillness and joy, do come. But it would be incorrect to say that we are practicing to make these experiences happen or that having more of them is better than having fewer of them.

The spirit of mindfulness is to practice for its own sake, and just to take each moment as it comes—pleasant or unpleasant, good, bad, or ugly—and then work with that because it is what is present now. With this attitude, life itself becomes practice. Then, rather than doing practice, it might better be said that the practice is doing you, or that life itself becomes your meditation teacher and your guide.

You Don't Have to Go Out of Your Way to Practice

Henry David Thoreau's two years at Walden Pond were above all a personal experiment in mindfulness. He chose to put his life on the line in order to revel in the wonder and simplicity of present moments. But you don't have to go out of your way or find someplace special to practice mindfulness. It is sufficient to make a little time in your life for stillness and what we call non-doing, and then tune in to your breathing.

All of Walden Pond is within your breath. The miracle of the changing seasons is within the breath; your parents and your children are within the breath; your body and your mind are within the breath. The breath is the current connecting body and mind, connecting us with our parents and our children, connecting our body with the outer world's body. It is the current of life. There are nothing but golden fish in this stream. All we need to see them clearly is the lens of awareness.

*

Time is but the stream I go a-fishing in. I drink at it; but while I drink, I see the sandy bottom and detect how shallow it is. Its thin current slides away, but eternity remains. I would drink deeper; fish in the sky, whose bottom is pebbly with stars.

THOREAU, *Walden*

*

In eternity there is indeed something true and sublime. But all these times and places and occasions are now and here. God himself culminates in the present moment, and will never be more divine in the lapse of all the ages.

THOREAU, *Walden*

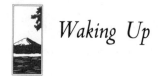# Waking Up

Taking up a formal meditation practice by making some time for it each day doesn't mean that you won't be able to think any more, or that you can't run around or get things done. It means that you are more likely to know what you are doing because you have stopped for a while and watched, listened, understood.

Thoreau saw this ever so clearly at Walden Pond. His closing message: "Only that day dawns to which we are awake." If we are to grasp the reality of our life while we have it, we will need to wake up to our moments. Otherwise, whole days, even a whole life, could slip past unnoticed.

One practical way to do this is to look at other people and ask yourself if you are really seeing them or just your thoughts about them. Sometimes our thoughts act like dream glasses. When we have them on, we see dream children, dream husband, dream wife, dream job, dream colleagues, dream partners, dream friends. We can live in a dream present for a dream future. Without knowing it, we are coloring everything, putting our spin on it all. While things in the dream may change and give the illusion of being vivid and real, it is still a dream we are caught in. But if we take off the glasses, maybe, just maybe, we might see a little more accurately what is actually here.

Thoreau felt the need to go off on a solitary retreat for an extended period of time (he stayed two years and two months at Walden Pond) to do this. "I went to the woods because I wished to live deliberately, to front only the essential facts of life, and see if I could not learn what it had to teach, and not, when I came to die, discover that I had not lived."

His deepest conviction: "To affect the quality of the day, that is the highest of arts. . . . I have never yet met a man who was quite awake. How could I have looked him in the face?"

TRY: Asking yourself from time to time, "Am I awake now?"

✤

My inside, listen to me, the greatest spirit,
the Teacher, is near,
wake up, wake up!

Run to his feet—
he is standing close to your head right now.
You have slept for millions and millions of years.
Why not wake up this morning?

KABIR

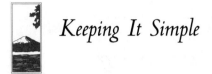

Keeping It Simple

If you do decide to start meditating, there's no need to tell other people about it, or talk about why you are doing it or what it's doing for you. In fact, there is no better way to waste your nascent energy and enthusiasm for practice and thwart your efforts so they will be unable to gather momentum. Best to meditate without advertising it.

Every time you get a strong impulse to talk about meditation and how wonderful it is, or how hard it is, or what it's doing for you these days, or what it's not, or you want to convince someone else how wonderful it would be for them, just look at it as more thinking and go meditate some more. The impulse will pass and everybody will be better off—especially you.

You Can't Stop the Waves but
You Can Learn to Surf

It is a commonly held view that meditation is a way to shut off the pressures of the world or of your own mind, but this is not an accurate impression. Meditation is neither shutting things out nor off. It is seeing things clearly, and deliberately positioning yourself differently in relationship to them.

People who come to our clinic quickly learn that stress is an inevitable part of life. While it is true that we can learn, by making intelligent choices, not to make things worse for ourselves in certain ways, there are many things in life over which we have little or no control. Stress is part of life, part of being human, intrinsic to the human condition itself. But that does not mean that we have to be victims in the face of large forces in our lives. We can learn to work with them, understand them, find meaning in them, make critical choices, and use their energies to grow in strength, wisdom, and compassion. A willingness to embrace and work with what is lies at the core of all meditation practice.

One way to envision how mindfulness works is to think of your mind as the surface of a lake or of the ocean. There are always waves on the water. Sometimes they are big, sometimes they are small, and sometimes they are almost imperceptible. The water's waves are churned up by winds, which come and go and vary in direction and intensity, just as do the winds of stress and change in our lives, which stir up waves in our minds.

People who don't understand meditation think that it is some kind of special inner manipulation which will magically shut off these waves so that the mind's surface will be flat, peaceful, and tranquil. But just as you can't put a glass plate on the water to calm the waves, so you can't artificially suppress the waves of your mind, and it is not too smart to try. It will only create more tension and inner struggle, not calmness. That doesn't mean that calmness is unattainable. It's just that it cannot be attained by misguided attempts to suppress the mind's natural activity.

It is possible through meditation to find shelter from much of the wind that agitates the mind. Over time, a good deal of the turbulence may die down from lack of continuous feeding. But ultimately the winds of life and of the mind will blow, do what we may. Meditation is about knowing something about this and how to work with it.

The spirit of mindfulness practice was nicely captured in a poster of a seventy-ish yogi, Swami Satchitananda, in full white beard and flowing robes atop a surfboard riding the waves off a Hawaiian beach. The caption read: "You can't stop the waves, but you can learn to surf."

Can Anybody Meditate?

I get asked this question a lot. I suspect people ask because they think that probably everybody else can meditate but they can't. They want to be reassured that they are not alone, that there are at least some other people they can identify with, those hapless souls who were born incapable of meditating. But it isn't so simple.

Thinking you are unable to meditate is a little like thinking you are unable to breathe, or to concentrate or relax. Pretty much everybody can breathe easily. And under the right circumstances, pretty much anybody can concentrate, anybody can relax.

People often confuse meditation with relaxation or some other special state that you have to get to or feel. When once or twice you try and you don't get anywhere or you didn't feel anything special, then you think you are one of those people who can't do it.

But, meditation is not about feeling a certain way. It's about feeling the way you feel. It's not about making the mind empty or still, although stillness does deepen in meditation and can be cultivated systematically. Above all, meditation is about letting the mind be as it is and knowing something about *how* it is in this moment. It's not about getting somewhere else, but about

33

allowing yourself to be where you already are. If you don't understand this, you will think you are constitutionally unable to meditate. But that's just more thinking, and in this case, incorrect thinking at that.

True, meditation does require energy and a commitment to stick with it. But then, wouldn't it be more accurate to say, "I won't stick with it," rather than, "I can't do it"? Anybody can sit down and watch their breath or watch their mind. And you don't have to be sitting. You could do it walking, standing, lying down, standing on one leg, running, or taking a bath. But to stay at it for even five minutes requires intentionality. To make it part of your life requires some discipline. So when people say they can't meditate, what they really mean is that they won't make time for it, or that when they try, they don't like what happens. It isn't what they are looking for or hoping for. It doesn't fulfill their expectations. So maybe they should try again, this time letting go of their expectations and just watching.

In Praise of Non-Doing

If you sit down to meditate, even for a moment, it will be a time for non-doing. It is very important not to think that this non-doing is synonymous with doing nothing. They couldn't be more different. Consciousness and intention matter here. In fact, they are key.

On the surface, it seems as if there might be two kinds of non-doing, one involving not doing any outward work, the other involving what we might call effortless activity. Ultimately we come to see that they are the same. It is the inward experience that counts here. What we frequently call formal meditation involves purposefully making a time for stopping all outward activity and cultivating stillness, with no agenda other than being fully present in each moment. Not doing anything. Perhaps such moments of non-doing are the greatest gift one can give oneself.

Thoreau would often sit in his doorway for hours and just watch, just listen, as the sun moved across the sky and the light and shadows changed imperceptibly:

*

There were times when I could not afford to sacrifice the bloom of the present moment to any work,

35

whether of the head or hand. I love a broad margin to my life. Sometimes, in a summer morning, having taken my accustomed bath, I sat in my sunny doorway from sunrise till noon, rapt in a revery, amidst the pines and hickories and sumachs, in undisturbed solitude and stillness, while the birds sang around or flitted noiseless though the house, until by the sun falling in at my west window, or the noise of some traveller's wagon on the distant highway, I was reminded of the lapse of time. I grew in those seasons like corn in the night, and they were far better than any work of the hands would have been. They were not time subtracted from my life, but so much over and above my usual allowance. I realized what the Orientals mean by contemplation and the forsaking of works. For the most part, I minded not how the hours went. The day advanced as if to light some work of mine; it was morning, and lo, now it is evening, and nothing memorable is accomplished. Instead of singing, like the birds, I silently smiled at my incessant good fortune. As the sparrow had its trill, sitting on the hickory before my door, so I had my chuckle or suppressed warble which he might hear out of my nest.

THOREAU, *Walden*

TRY: Recognizing the bloom of the present moment in your daily meditation practice if you have one. If you are up early in the morning, try going outside and looking (a sustained, mindful, attentive looking) at the stars, at the moon, at the dawning light when it comes. Feel the air, the cold, the warmth (a sustained, mindful, attentive feeling). Realize that the world around you is sleeping. Remember when you see the stars that you are looking back in time millions of years. The past is present now and here.

Then go and sit or meditate lying down. Let this or any time you practice be your time for letting go of all doing, for shifting into the being mode, in which you simply dwell in stillness and mindfulness, attending to the moment-to-moment unfolding of the present, adding nothing, subtracting nothing, affirming that "This is it."

The Non-Doing Paradox

The flavor and the sheer joy of non-doing are difficult for Americans to grasp because our culture places so much value on doing and on progress. Even our leisure tends to be busy and mindless. The joy of non-doing is that nothing else needs to happen for *this* moment to be complete. The wisdom in it, and the equanimity that comes out of it, lie in knowing that something else surely will.

When Thoreau says, "it was morning, and lo, now it is evening, and nothing memorable is accomplished," this is waving a red flag in front of a bull for go-getting, progress-oriented people. But who is to say that his realizations of one morning spent in his doorway are less memorable or have less merit than a lifetime of busyness, lived with scant appreciation for stillness and the bloom of the present moment?

Thoreau was singing a song which needed hearing then as it does now. He is, to this day, continually pointing out, for anyone willing to listen, the deep importance of contemplation and of non-attachment to any result other than the sheer enjoyment of being, all "far better than any work of the hands would have been." This view recalls the old Zen master who said, "Ho ho. For forty years I have been selling water by the river and my efforts are totally without merit."

It reeks of paradox. The only way you can do anything of value is to have the effort come out of non-doing and to let go of caring whether it will be of use or not. Otherwise, self-involvement and greediness can sneak in and distort your relationship to the work, or the work itself, so that it is off in some way, biased, impure, and ultimately not completely satisfying, even if it is good. Good scientists know this mind state and guard against it because it inhibits the creative process and distorts one's ability to see connections clearly.

Non-Doing in Action

Non-doing can arise within action as well as in stillness. The inward stillness of the doer merges with the outward activity to such an extent that the action does itself. Effortless activity. Nothing is forced. There is no exertion of the will, no small-minded "I," "me," or "mine" to lay claim to a result, yet nothing is left undone. Non-doing is a cornerstone of mastery in any realm of activity. Here's a classic statement of it from third-century China:

> Prince Wen Hui's cook
> Was cutting up an ox.
> Out went a hand,
> Down went a shoulder,
> He planted a foot,
> He pressed with a knee,
> The ox fell apart
> With a whisper,
> The bright cleaver murmured
> Like a gentle wind.
> Rhythm! Timing!
> Like a sacred dance,

Like "The Mulberry Grove,"
Like ancient harmonies!

"Good work!" the Prince exclaimed,
"Your method is faultless!"
"Method?" said the cook
Laying aside his cleaver,
"What I follow is Tao
Beyond all methods!

"When I first began
To cut up oxen
I would see before me
The whole ox
All in one mass.
After three years
I no longer saw this mass.
I saw the distinctions.

"But now I see nothing
With the eye. My whole being
Apprehends.
My senses are idle. The spirit
Free to work without plan
Follows its own instinct
Guided by natural line,

By the secret opening, the hidden space,
My cleaver finds its own way.
I cut through no joint, chop no bone.

. . .

"There are spaces in the joints;
The blade is thin and keen:
When this thinness
Finds that space
There is all the room you need!
It goes like a breeze!
Hence I have this cleaver nineteen years
As if newly sharpened!

"True, there are sometimes
Tough joints. I feel them coming,
I slow down, I watch closely,
Hold back, barely move the blade,
And whump! the part falls away
Landing like a clod of earth.

"Then I withdraw the blade,
I stand still
And let the joy of the work
Sink in.
I clean the blade
And put it away."

Prince Wen Hui said,
"This is it! My cook has shown me
How I ought to live
My own life!"

CHUANG TZU

Doing Non-Doing

Non-doing has nothing to do with being indolent or passive. Quite the contrary. It takes great courage and energy to cultivate non-doing, both in stillness and in activity. Nor is it easy to make a special time for non-doing and to keep at it in the face of everything in our lives which needs to be done.

But non-doing doesn't have to be threatening to people who feel they always have to get things done. They might find they get even more "done," and done better, by practicing non-doing. Non-doing simply means letting things be and allowing them to unfold in their own way. Enormous effort can be involved, but it is a graceful, knowledgeable, effortless effort, a "doerless doing," cultivated over a lifetime.

Effortless activity happens at moments in dance and in sports at the highest levels of performance; when it does, it takes everybody's breath away. But it also happens in every area of human activity, from painting to car repair to parenting. Years of practice and experience combine on some occasions, giving rise to a new capacity to let execution unfold beyond technique, beyond exertion, beyond thinking. Action then becomes a pure expression of art, of being, of letting go of all doing—a merging of mind and body in motion. We thrill in watching a superb performance, whether athletic or artistic, because it allows us to participate in the magic of true mastery, to be uplifted, if only briefly, and perhaps to share in the intention that each of us, in our own way, might touch such moments of grace and harmony in the living of our own lives.

Thoreau said, "To affect the quality of the day, that is the highest of arts." Martha Graham, speaking of the art of dance, put it this way: "All that is important is this one moment in movement. Make the moment vital and worth living. Do not let it slip away unnoticed and unused."

No meditation masters could have spoken truer. We can apprentice ourselves to this work, knowing full well that non-doing is truly the work of a lifetime; and conscious all the while that the doing mode is usually so strong in us that the cultivating of non-doing ironically takes considerable effort.

Meditation is synonymous with the practice of non-doing. We aren't practicing to make things perfect or to do things perfectly. Rather, we practice to grasp and realize (make real for ourselves) the fact that things already are perfect, perfectly what they are. This has everything to do with holding the present moment in its fullness without imposing anything extra on it, perceiving its purity and the freshness of its potential to give rise to the next moment. Then, knowing what is what, seeing as clearly as possible, and conscious of not knowing more than we actually do, we act, make a move, take a stand, take a chance.

Some people speak of this as flow, one moment flowing seamlessly, effortlessly into the next, cradled in the streambed of mindfulness.

T R Y: During the day, see if you can detect the bloom of the present moment in every moment, the ordinary ones, the "in-between" ones, even the hard ones. Work at allowing more things to unfold in your life without forcing them to happen and without rejecting the ones that don't fit your idea of what "should" be happening. See if you can sense the "spaces" through which you might move with no effort in the spirit of Chuang Tzu's cook. Notice how if you can make some time early in the day for being, with no agenda, it can change the quality of the rest of your day. By affirming first what is primary in your own being, see if you don't get a mindful jump on the whole day and wind up more capable of sensing, appreciating, and responding to the bloom of each moment.

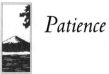# *Patience*

Certain attitudes or mental qualities support meditation practice and provide a rich soil in which the seeds of mindfulness can flourish. By purposefully cultivating these qualities, we are actually tilling the soil of our own mind and ensuring that it can serve as a source of clarity, compassion, and right action in our lives.

These inner qualities which support meditation practice cannot be imposed, legislated, or decreed. They can only be *cultivated*, and this only when you have reached the point where your inner motivation is strong enough to want to cease contributing to your own suffering and confusion and perhaps to that of others. It amounts to behaving ethically—a sorely maligned concept in many circles.

On the radio, I heard someone define ethics as "obedience to the unenforceable." Not bad. You do it for inner reasons, not because someone is keeping score, or because you might be punished if you break the rules and get caught. You are marching to the beat of your own drummer. It is an inner hearing you are attending to, just as it is an inner soil that is being tilled for the cultivation of mindfulness. But you cannot have harmony without a commitment to ethical behavior. It's the fence that keeps out the goats that will eat all the young shoots in your garden.

I see patience as one of these fundamental ethical attitudes. If you cultivate patience, you almost can't help cultivating mindfulness, and your meditation practice will gradually become richer and more mature. After all, if you really aren't trying to get anywhere else in this moment, patience takes care of itself. It is a remembering that things unfold in their own time. The seasons cannot be hurried. Spring comes, the grass grows by itself. Being in a hurry usually doesn't help, and it can create a great deal of suffering—sometimes in us, sometimes in those who have to be around us.

Patience is an ever present alternative to the mind's endemic restlessness and impatience. Scratch the surface of impatience and what you will find lying beneath it, subtly or not so subtly, is anger. It's the strong energy of not wanting things to be the way they are and blaming someone (often yourself) or something for it. This doesn't mean you can't hurry when you have to. It is possible even to hurry patiently, mindfully, moving fast because you have chosen to.

From the perspective of patience, things happen because other things happen. Nothing is separate and isolated. There is no absolute, end-of-the-line, the-buck-stops-here root cause. If someone hits you with a stick, you don't get angry at the stick or at the arm that swung it; you get angry at the person attached to the arm. But if you look a little deeper, you can't find a satisfactory root cause or place for your anger even in the person, who literally doesn't know what he is doing and is therefore out of his mind at that moment. Where should the blame lie, or the punishment? Maybe we should be angry at the person's parents for the abuse they may have showered on a defenseless child. Or maybe at the world for its lack of compassion. But what is the world? Are you not a part of that world? Do not you yourself have angry impulses and under some conditions find yourself in touch with violent, even murderous impulses?

The Dalai Lama shows no anger toward the Chinese, even though the policy of the Chinese government for years has been to practice genocide toward Tibetans, culturicide toward their institutions, beliefs, and everything they hold dear, and geocide toward the very land they live on. When asked about his apparent lack of anger toward the Chinese by an incredulous reporter at the time he won the Nobel Peace Prize, the Dalai Lama replied something to the effect that: "They have taken everything from us; should I let them take my mind as well?"

This attitude is itself a remarkable display of peace . . . the inner peace of knowing what is most fundamental, and the outer peace of embodying that wisdom in carriage and action. Peace, and a willingness to be patient in the face of such enormous provocation and suffering, can only come about through the inner cultivation of compassion, a compassion that is not limited to friends, but is felt equally for those who, out of ignorance and often seen as evil, may cause you and those you love to suffer.

That degree of selfless compassion is based on what Buddhists call "right mindfulness" and "right understanding." It doesn't just spring up spontaneously. It needs to be practiced, cultivated. It's not that feelings of anger don't arise. It's that the anger can be used, worked with, harnessed so that its energies can nourish patience, compassion, harmony, and wisdom in ourselves and perhaps in others as well.

In taking up meditation, we are cultivating the quality of patience every time we stop and sit and become aware of the flow of our own breathing. And this invitation to ourselves to be more open, more in touch, more patient with our moments naturally extends itself to other times in our lives as well. We know that things unfold according to their own nature. We can remember to let our lives unfold in the same way. We don't have to let our anxieties and our desire for certain results dominate the quality of the moment, even when things are painful. When we have to push, we push. When we have to pull, we pull. But we know when not to push too, and when not to pull.

Through it all, we attempt to bring balance to the present moment, understanding that in patience lies wisdom, knowing that what will come next will be determined in large measure by how we are now. This is helpful to keep in mind when we get impatient in our meditation practice, or when we get frustrated, impatient, and angry in our lives.

*

Do you have the patience to wait
till your mud settles and the water is clear?
Can you remain unmoving
till the right action arises by itself?

LAO-TZU, *Tao-te-Ching*

*

I exist as I am, that is enough,
If no other in the world be aware I sit content,
And if each and all be aware I sit content.

One world is aware, and by far the largest to me, and that
is myself,
And whether I come to my own today or in ten thousand
or ten million years,
I can cheerfully take it now, or with equal cheerfulness,
I can wait.

WALT WHITMAN, *Leaves of Grass*

T R Y : Looking into impatience and anger when they arise. See if you can adopt a different perspective, one which sees things as unfolding in their own time. This is especially useful when you are feeling under pressure and blocked or stymied in something you want or need to do. Hard as it may seem, try not to push the river in that moment but listen carefully to it instead. What does it tell you? What is it telling you to do? If nothing, then just breathe, let things be as they are, let go into patience, continue listening. If the river tells you something, then do it, but do it mindfully. Then pause, wait patiently, listen again.

As you attend the gentle flow of your own breathing during times of formal meditation practice, notice the occasional pull of the mind to get on to something else, to want to fill up your time or change what is happening. Instead of losing yourself at these times, try to sit patiently with the breath and with a keen awareness of what is unfolding in each moment, allowing it to unfold as it will, without imposing anything on it . . . just watching, just breathing . . . embodying stillness, becoming patience.

Letting Go

The phrase "letting go" has to be high in the running for New Age cliché of the century. It is overused, abused daily. Yet it is such a powerful inward maneuver that it merits looking into, cliché or no. There is something vitally important to be learned from the practice of letting go.

Letting go means just what it says. It's an invitation to cease clinging to anything—whether it be an idea, a thing, an event, a particular time, or view, or desire. It is a conscious decision to release with full acceptance into the stream of present moments as they are unfolding. To let go means to give up coercing, resisting, or struggling, in exchange for something more powerful and wholesome which comes out of allowing things to be as they are without getting caught up in your attraction to or rejection of them, in the intrinsic stickiness of wanting, of liking and disliking. It's akin to letting your palm open to unhand something you have been holding on to.

But it's not only the stickiness of our desires concerning outer events which catches us. Nor is it only a holding on with our hands. We hold on with our minds. We catch *ourselves,* get stuck *ourselves,* by holding, often desperately, to narrow views, to self-serving hopes and wishes. Letting go really refers to choosing to become transparent to the strong pull of our own likes and dislikes, and of the unawareness that draws us to cling to them. To be transparent requires that we allow fears and insecurities to play themselves out in the field of full awareness.

Letting go is only possible if we can bring awareness and acceptance to the nitty-gritty of just how stuck we can get, if we allow ourselves to recognize the lenses we slip so unconsciously between observer and observed that then filter and color, bend and shape our view. We can open in those sticky moments, especially if we are able to capture them in awareness and recognize it when we get caught up in either pursuing and clinging or condemning and rejecting in seeking our own gain.

Stillness, insight, and wisdom arise only when we can settle into being complete in this moment, without having to seek or hold on to or reject anything. This is a testable proposition. Try it out just for fun. See for yourself whether letting go when a part of you really wants to hold on doesn't bring a deeper satisfaction than clinging.

Non-Judging

It doesn't take long in meditation to discover that part of our mind is constantly evaluating our experiences, comparing them with other experiences or holding them up against expectations and standards that we create, often out of fear. Fear that I'm not good enough, that bad things will happen, that good things won't last, that other people might hurt me, that I won't get my way, that only I know anything, that I'm the only one who doesn't know anything. We tend to see things through tinted glasses: through the lens of whether something is good for me or bad for me, or whether or not it conforms to my beliefs or philosophy. If it is good, I like it. If it is bad, I don't like it. If it is neither, I have no feelings about it one way or the other, and may hardly notice it at all.

When you dwell in stillness, the judging mind can come through like a foghorn. I don't like the pain in my knee. . . . This is boring. . . . I like this feeling of stillness; I had a good meditation yesterday, but today I'm having a bad meditation. . . . It's not working for me. I'm no good at this. I'm no good, period. This type of thinking dominates the mind and weighs it down. It's like carrying around a suitcase full of rocks on your head. It feels good to put it down. Imagine how it might feel to suspend all your judging and instead to let each moment be just as it is, without attempting to evaluate it as "good" or "bad." This would be a true stillness, a true liberation.

Meditation means cultivating a non-judging attitude toward what comes up in the mind, come what may. Without it, you are not practicing meditation. That doesn't mean judging won't be going on. Of course it will, because it is in the very nature of the mind to compare and judge and evaluate. When it occurs, we don't try to stop it or ignore it, any more than we would try to stop any other thoughts that might come through our mind.

The tack we take in meditation is simply to witness whatever comes up in the mind or the body and to recognize it without condemning it or pursuing it, knowing that our judgments are unavoidable and necessarily limiting thoughts *about* experience. What we are interested in in meditation is direct contact with the experience itself—whether it is of an inbreath, an outbreath, a sensation or feeling, a sound, an impulse, a thought, a perception, or a judgment. And we remain attentive to the possibility of getting caught up in judging the judging itself, or in labeling some judgments good and others bad.

While our thinking colors all our experience, more often than not our thoughts tend to be less than completely accurate. Usually they are merely uninformed private opinions, reactions and prejudices based on limited knowledge and influenced primarily by our past conditioning. All the same, when not recognized as such and named, our thinking can prevent us from seeing clearly in the present moment. We get caught up in *thinking* we know what we are seeing and feeling, and in project-ing our judgments out onto everything we see off a hairline trigger. Just being familiar with this deeply entrenched pattern and watching it as it happens can lead to greater non-judgmental receptivity and acceptance.

A non-judging orientation certainly does not mean that you cease knowing how to act or behave responsibly in society, or that anything anybody does is okay. It simply means that we can act with much greater clarity in our own lives, and be more balanced, more effective, and more ethical in our activities, if we know that we are immersed in a stream of unconscious liking and disliking which screens us from the world and from the basic purity of our own being. The mind states of liking and disliking can take up permanent residency in us, unconsciously feeding addictive behaviors in all domains of life. When we are able to recognize and name the seeds of greediness or craving, however subtle, in the mind's constant wanting and pursuing of the things or results that we like, and the seeds of aversion or hatred in our rejecting or maneuvering to avoid the things we don't like, that stops us for a moment and reminds us that such forces really are at work in our own minds to one extent or another almost all the time. It's no exaggeration to say that they have a chronic, viral-like toxicity that prevents us from seeing things as they actually are and mobilizing our true potential.

Trust

Trust is a feeling of confidence or conviction that things can unfold within a dependable framework that embodies order and integrity. We may not always understand what is happening to us, or to another, or what is occurring in a particular situation; but if we trust ourselves, or another, or we place our trust in a process or an ideal, we can find a powerful stabilizing element embracing security, balance, and openness within the trusting which, in some way, if not based on naivete, intuitively guides us and protects us from harm or self-destruction.

The feeling state of trust is important to cultivate in mindfulness practice, for if we do not trust in our ability to observe, to be open and attentive, to reflect upon experience, to grow and learn from observing and attending, to know something deeply, we will hardly persevere in cultivating any of these abilities, and so they will only wither or lie dormant.

Part of mindfulness practice is to cultivate a trusting heart. Let's begin by looking deeply into what we can trust in ourselves. If we don't immediately know what there is to trust in ourselves, maybe we need to look a little deeper, to dwell a little longer with ourselves in stillness and in simply being. If we are unaware of what we are doing a good deal of the time, and we don't particularly like the way things turn out in our lives, perhaps it's time to pay closer attention, to be more in touch, to observe the choices we make and their consequences down the road.

Perhaps we could experiment with trusting the present moment, accepting whatever we feel or think or see in *this* moment because this is what is present now. If we can take a stand here, and let go into the full texture of now, we may find that this very moment is worthy of our trust. From such experiments, conducted over and over again, may come a new sense that somewhere deep within us resides a profoundly healthy and trustworthy core, and that our intuitions, as deep resonances of the actuality of the present moment, are worthy of our trust.

*

Be strong then, and enter into your own body;
there you have a solid place for your feet.
Think about it carefully!
Don't go off somewhere else!
Kabir says this: just throw away all thoughts of
 imaginary things,
and stand firm in that which you are.

KABIR

Generosity

Generosity is another quality which, like patience, letting go, non-judging, and trust, provides a solid foundation for mindfulness practice. You might experiment with using the cultivation of generosity as a vehicle for deep self-observation and inquiry as well as an exercise in giving. A good place to start is with yourself. See if you can give yourself gifts that may be true blessings, such as self-acceptance, or some time each day with no purpose. Practice feeling deserving enough to accept these gifts without obligation—to simply receive from yourself, and from the universe.

> See if you can be in touch with a core within you which is rich beyond reckoning in all important ways. Let that core start radiating its energy outwardly, through your entire body, and beyond. Experiment with giving away this energy—in little ways at first—directing it toward yourself and toward others with no thought of gain or return. Give more than you think you can, trusting that you are richer than you think. Celebrate this richness. Give as if you had inexhaustible wealth. This is called "kingly giving."

I am not talking solely of money or material possessions, although it can be wonderfully growth-enhancing, uplifting, and truly helpful to share material abundance. Rather, what is being suggested here is that you practice sharing the fullness of your being, your best self, your enthusiasm, your vitality, your spirit, your trust, your openness, above all, your presence. Share it with yourself, with your family, with the world.

TRY: Noticing the resistance to the impulse to give, the worries about the future, the feeling that you may be giving too much, or the thought that it won't be appreciated "enough," or that you will be exhausted from the effort, or that you won't get anything out of it, or that you don't have enough yourself. Consider the possibility that none of these are actually true, but that they are just forms of inertia, constriction, and fear-based self-protection. These thoughts and feelings are the rough edges of self-cherishing, which rub up against the world and frequently cause us and others pain and a sense of distance, isolation, and diminishment. Giving sands down such rough edges and helps us become more mindful of our inner wealth. By practicing mindfulness of generosity, by giving, and by observing its effects on ourselves and others, we are transforming ourselves, purifying ourselves, discovering expanded versions of ourselves.

You may protest that you don't have enough energy or enthusiasm to give *anything* away, that you are already feeling overwhelmed, or impoverished. Or you may feel that all you do is give, give, give, and that it is just taken for granted by others, not appreciated or even seen, or that you use it as a way of hiding from pain and fear, as a way of making sure others like you or feel dependent on you. Such difficult patterns and relationships themselves call out for attention and careful scrutiny. Mindless giving is never healthy or generous. It is important to understand your motives for giving, and to know when some kinds of giving are not a display of generosity but rather of fear and lack of confidence.

In the mindful cultivation of generosity, it is not necessary to give everything away, or even anything. Above all, generosity is an inward giving, a feeling state, a willingness to share your own being with the world. Most important is to trust and honor your instincts but, at the same time, to walk the edge and take some risks as part of your experiment. Perhaps you need to give less, or to trust your intuition about exploitation or unhealthy motives or impulses. Perhaps you do need to give, but in a different way, or to different people. Perhaps most of all, you need to give to *yourself* first for a while. Then you might try giving others a tiny bit more than you think you can, consciously noting and letting go of any ideas of getting anything in return.

Initiate giving. Don't wait for someone to ask. See what happens—especially to you. You may find that you gain a greater clarity about yourself and about your relationships, as well as more energy rather than less. You may find that, rather than exhausting yourself or your resources, you will replenish them. Such is the power of mindful, selfless generosity. At the deepest level, there is no giver, no gift, and no recipient . . . only the universe rearranging itself.

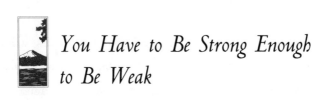

You Have to Be Strong Enough to Be Weak

If you are a strong-willed and accomplished person, you may often give the impression that you are invulnerable to feeling inadequate or insecure or hurt. This can be very isolating and ultimately cause you and others great pain. Other people will be all too happy to take in that impression and to collude in propagating it by projecting a Rock of Gibraltar persona onto you which doesn't allow you to have any real feelings. In fact, you can all too easily get out of touch with your own true feelings behind the intoxicating shield of image and aura. This isolation happens a lot to fathers in the nuclear family and to people in positions of relative power everywhere.

Thinking of yourself as getting stronger through the meditation practice can create a similar dilemma. You can start believing in and acting out the part of the supremely invulnerable, correct meditator—one who has everything under control and is wise enough to deal with everything without being caught up in reactive emotions. In the process, you can cleverly arrest your own development without even knowing it. We all have an emotional life. We wall ourselves off from it at our own peril.

So, when you notice yourself building up an image of invincibility, or strength, or special knowledge, or wisdom based on your meditative experiences, thinking perhaps that you're getting somewhere in your practice, and you start talking a lot about meditation in a way that is self-promotional and inflationary, it's a good idea to bring mindfulness to that mind-set and to ask yourself whether you are running from your vulnerability, or perhaps from grief you may be carrying, or from fear of some sort. If you are truly strong, there is little need to emphasize it to yourself or to others. Best to take another tack entirely and direct your attention where you fear most to look. You can do this by allowing yourself to feel, even to cry, to not have to have opinions about everything, to not appear invincible or unfeeling to others, but instead to be in touch with and appropriately open about your feelings. What looks like weakness is actually where your strength lies. And what looks like strength is often weakness, an attempt to cover up fear; this is an act or a facade, however convincing it might appear to others or even to yourself.

T R Y : Recognizing the ways in which you meet obstacles with harshness. Experiment with being soft when your impulse is to be hard, generous when your impulse is to be withholding, open when your impulse is to close up or shut down emotionally. When there is grief or sadness, try letting it be here. Allow yourself to feel whatever you are feeling. Notice any labels you attach to crying or feeling vulnerable. Let go of the labels. Just feel what you are feeling, all the while cultivating moment-to-moment awareness, riding the waves of "up" and "down," "good" and "bad," "weak" and "strong," until you see that they are all inadequate to fully describe your experience. Be with the experience itself. Trust in your deepest strength of all: to be present, to be wakeful.

Voluntary Simplicity

The impulse frequently arises in me to squeeze another this or another that into this moment. Just this phone call, just stopping off here on my way there. Never mind that it might be in the opposite direction.

I've learned to identify this impulse and mistrust it. I work hard at saying no to it. It would have me eat breakfast with my eyes riveted to the cereal box, reading for the hundredth time the dietary contents of the contents, or the amazing free offer from the company. This impulse doesn't care what it feeds on, as long as it's feeding. The newspaper is an even better draw, or the L. L. Bean catalogue, or whatever else is around. It scavenges to fill time, conspires with my mind to keep me unconscious, lulled in a fog of numbness to a certain extent, just enough to fill or overfill my belly while I actually miss breakfast. It has me unavailable to others at those times, missing the play of light on the table, the smells in the room, the energies of the moment, including arguments and disputes, as we come together before going our separate ways for the day.

I like to practice voluntary simplicity to counter such impulses and make sure nourishment comes at a deep level. It involves intentionally doing only one thing at a time and making sure I am here for it. Many occasions present themselves: taking a walk, for instance, or spending a few moments with the dog in which I am really with the dog. Voluntary simplicity means going fewer places in one day rather than more, seeing less so I can see more, doing less so I can do more, acquiring less so I can have more. It all ties in. It's not a real option for me as a father of young children, a breadwinner, a husband, an oldest son to my parents, a person who cares deeply about his work to go off to one Walden Pond or another and sit under a tree for a few years, listening to the grass grow and the seasons change, much as the impulse beckons at times. But within the organized chaos and complexity of family life and work, with all their demands and responsibilities, frustrations and unsurpassed gifts, there is ample opportunity for choosing simplicity in small ways.

Slowing everything down is a big part of this. Telling my mind and body to stay put with my daughter rather than answering the phone, not reacting to inner impulses to call someone who "needs calling" right in that moment, choosing not to acquire new things on impulse, or even to automatically answer the siren call of magazines or television or movies on the first ring are all ways to simplify one's life a little. Others are maybe just to sit for an evening and do nothing, or to read a book, or go for a walk alone or with a child or with my wife, to restack the woodpile or look at the moon, or feel the air on my face under the trees, or go to sleep early.

I practice saying no to keep my life simple, and I find I never do it enough. It's an arduous discipline all its own, and well worth the effort. Yet it is also tricky. There are needs and opportunities to which one must respond. A commitment to simplicity in the midst of the world is a delicate balancing act. It is always in need of retuning, further inquiry, attention. But I find the notion of voluntary simplicity keeps me mindful of what is important, of an ecology of mind and body and world in which everything is interconnected and every choice has far-reaching consequences. You don't get to control it all. But choosing simplicity whenever possible adds to life an element of deepest freedom which so easily eludes us, and many opportunities to discover that less may actually be more.

*

Simplicity, simplicity, simplicity! I say let your affairs be as two or three, and not a hundred or a thousand; instead of a million count half a dozen. . . . In the midst of this chopping sea of civilized life, such are the clouds and storms and quicksands and the thousand-and-one items to be allowed for, that a man has to live, if he would not founder and go to the bottom and not make his port at all, by dead reckoning, and he must be a great calculator indeed who succeeds. Simplify, Simplify.

THOREAU, Walden

Concentration

Concentration is a cornerstone of mindfulness practice. Your mindfulness will only be as robust as the capacity of your mind to be calm and stable. Without calmness, the mirror of mindfulness will have an agitated and choppy surface, and will not be able to reflect things with any accuracy.

Concentration can be practiced either hand in hand with mindfulness or separately. You can think of concentration as the capacity of the mind to sustain an unwavering attention on one object of observation. It is cultivated by attending to one thing, such as the breath, and just limiting one's focus to that. In Sanskrit, concentration is called *samadhi,* or "onepointedness." Samadhi is developed and deepened by continually bringing the attention back to the breath every time it wanders. When practicing strictly concentrative forms of meditation, we purposefully refrain from any efforts to inquire into areas such as where the mind went when it wandered off, or that the quality of the breath fluctuates. Our energy is directed solely toward experiencing *this* breath coming in, *this* breath going out, or some other single object of attention. With extended practice, the mind tends to become better and better at staying on the breath, or noticing even the earliest impulse to become distracted by something else, and either resisting its pull in the first place and staying on the breath, or quickly returning to it.

A calmness develops with intensive concentration practice that has a remarkably stable quality to it. It is steadfast, profound, hard to disturb, no matter what comes up. It is a great gift to oneself to be able periodically to cultivate samadhi over an extended period of time. This is most readily accomplished on long, silent meditation retreats, when one can withdraw from the world à la Thoreau for this very purpose.

The stability and calmness which come with onepointed concentration practice form the foundation for the cultivation of mindfulness. Without some degree of samadhi, your mindfulness will not be very strong. You can only look deeply into something if you can sustain your looking without being constantly thrown off by distractions or by the agitation of your own mind. The deeper your concentration, the deeper the potential for mindfulness.

The experience of deep samadhi is very pleasant. In attending to the breath with onepointed concentration, everything else falls away—including thoughts, feelings, the outside world. Samadhi is characterized by absorption in stillness and undisturbed peacefulness. A taste of this stillness can be attractive, even intoxicating. One naturally finds oneself seeking this peacefulness and the simplicity of a state characterized by absorption and bliss.

But concentration practice, however strong and satisfying, is incomplete without mindfulness to complement and deepen it. By itself, it resembles a state of withdrawal from the world. Its characteristic energy is closed rather than open, absorbed rather than available, trancelike rather than fully awake. What is missing is the energy of curiosity, inquiry, investigation, openness, availability, engagement with the full range of phenomena experienced by human beings. This is the domain of mindfulness practice, in which onepointedness and the ability to bring calmness and stability of mind to the present moment are put in the service of looking deeply into and understanding the interconnectedness of a wide range of life experiences.

Concentration can be of great value, but it can also be seriously limiting if you become seduced by the pleasant quality of this inner experience and come to see it as a refuge from life in an unpleasant and unsatisfactory world. You might be tempted to avoid the messiness of daily living for the tranquility of stillness and peacefulness. This of course would be an attachment to stillness, and like any strong attachment, it leads to delusion. It arrests development and short-circuits the cultivation of wisdom.

Vision

It is virtually impossible, and senseless anyway, to commit yourself to a daily meditation practice without some view of why you are doing it, what its value might be in your life, a sense of why this might be *your* way and not just another tilting at imaginary windmills. In traditional societies, this vision was supplied and continually reinforced by the culture. If you were a Buddhist, you might practice because the whole culture valued meditation as *the* path to clarity, compassion, and Buddhahood, a path of wisdom leading to the eradication of suffering. But in the Western cultural mainstream, you will find precious little support for choosing such a personal path of discipline and constancy, especially such an unusual one involving effort but non-doing, energy but no tangible "product." What is more, any superficial or romantic notions we might harbor of becoming a better person—more calm or more clear or more compassionate— don't endure for long when we face the turbulence of our lives, our minds and bodies, or even the prospect of getting up early in the morning when it is cold and dark to sit by yourself and be in the present moment. It's too easily put off or seen as trivial or of secondary importance, so it can always wait while you catch a little more sleep or at least stay warm in bed.

If you hope to bring meditation into your life in any kind of long-term, committed way, you will need a vision that is truly your own—one that is deep and tenacious and that lies close to the core of who you believe yourself to be, what you value in your life, and where you see yourself going. Only the strength of such a dynamic vision and the motivation from which it springs can possibly keep you on this path year in and year out, with a willingness to practice every day and to bring mindfulness to bear on whatever is happening, to open to whatever is perceived, and to let it point to where the holding is and where the letting go and the growing need to happen.

Meditation practice is hardly romantic. The ways in which we need to grow are usually those we are the most supremely defended against and are least willing to admit even exist, let alone take an undefended, mindful peek at and then act on to change. It won't be sustaining enough to have a quixotic idea of yourself as a meditator, or to hold the opinion that meditation is good for you because it has been good for others, or because Eastern wisdom sounds deep to you, or because you are in the habit of meditating. The vision we are speaking of has to be renewed every day, has to be right out front all the time, because mindfulness itself requires this level of awareness of purpose, of intention. Otherwise, we might as well stay in bed.

The practice itself has to become the daily embodiment of your vision and contain what you value most deeply. It doesn't mean trying to change or be different from how you are, calm when you're not feeling calm, or kind when you really feel angry.

Rather, it is bearing in mind what is most important to you so that it is not lost or betrayed in the heat and reactivity of a particular moment. If mindfulness is deeply important to you, then every moment is an opportunity to practice.

For example, suppose angry feelings come up at some point in your day. If you find yourself feeling angry and expressing it, you will also find yourself monitoring that expression and its effects moment by moment. You may be in touch with its validity as a feeling state, with the antecedent causes of your strong feeling, and the way it is coming out in your body gestures and stances, in your tone of voice, in your choice of words and arguments, as well as the impression it is making on others. There is much to be said for the conscious expression of anger, and it is well known medically and psychologically that suppressing anger in the sense of internalizing it is unhealthy, particularly if it becomes habitual. But it is also unhealthy to vent anger uncontrollably as a matter of habit and reaction, however "justifiable." You can feel it cloud the mind. It breeds feelings of aggression and violence—even if the anger is in the service of righting a wrong or getting something important to happen—and thus intrinsically warps what is, whether you are in the right or not. You can feel this even when you can't stop yourself sometimes. Mindfulness can put you in touch with the toxicity of the anger to yourself and to others. I always come away from it feeling that there is something inadequate about anger, even when I am objectively on high ground. Its innate toxicity taints all it touches. If its energy can be transmuted to forcefulness and wisdom, without the smoke and fire of self-absorption or self-righteousness, then its power multiplies, and so does its capacity to transform both the object of the anger and the source.

So, if you practice purposefully expanding the context of the anger (yours or someone else's) right in those very moments that it is arising and peaking, knowing that there must be something larger and more fundamental that you are forgetting in the heat of the emotion, then you can touch an awareness inside yourself which is not attached to or invested in the anger-fire. Awareness sees the anger; it knows the depth of the anger; and it is larger than the anger. It can therefore hold the anger the way a pot contains food. The pot of awareness helps us cradle the anger and see that it may be producing more harmful effects than beneficial ones, even if that is not our aim. In this way, it helps us cook the anger, digest the anger, so that we can *use* it effectively, and, in changing from an automatic reacting to a conscious responding, perhaps move beyond it altogether. This and other options stem from a careful listening to the dictates of the *whole* situation.

Our vision has to do with our values, and with our personal blueprint for what is most important in life. It has to do with first principles. If you believe in love, do you manifest it or just talk a lot? If you believe in compassion, in non-harming, in kindness, in wisdom, in generosity, in calmness, in solitude, in non-doing, in being even-handed and clear, do you manifest these qualities in your daily life? This is the level of intentionality which is required to keep your meditation practice vital, so that it doesn't succumb to becoming purely a mechanical exercise, driven only by the forces of habit or belief.

*

Renew thyself completely each day; do it again, and again, and forever again.

CHINESE INSCRIPTION CITED BY THOREAU IN Walden

T R Y : Asking yourself why you meditate or why you want to meditate. Don't believe your first answers. Just write down a list of whatever comes to mind. Continue asking yourself. Also, inquire about your values, about what you honor most in life. Make a list of what is really important to you. Ask yourself: What is my vision, my map for where I am and where I am going? Does this vision reflect my true values and intentions? Am I remembering to embody those values? Do I practice my intentions? How am I *now* in my job, in my family, in my relationships, with myself? How do I want to be? How might I live my vision, my values? How do I relate to suffering, both my own and others'?

Meditation Develops Full Human Beings

I'm told that in Pali, the original language of the Buddha, there is no one word corresponding to our word "meditation," even though meditation might be said to have evolved to an extraordinary degree in ancient Indian culture. One word that is frequently used is *bhavana*. Bhavana translates as "development through mental training." To me, this strikes the mark; meditation really is about human development. It is a natural extension of cutting teeth, growing an adult-sized body, working and making things happen in the world, raising a family, going into debt of one kind or another (even if only to yourself through bargains that may imprison the soul), and realizing that you too will grow old and die. At some time or another, you are practically forced to sit down and contemplate your life and question who you are and where the meaning lies in the journey of life . . . your life.

The old fairy tales, we are told by their modern interpreters, Bruno Bettelheim, Robert Bly, Joseph Campbell, and Clarissa Pinkola Estes, are ancient maps, offering their own guidance for the development of full human beings. The wisdom of these tales comes down to our day from a time before writing, having been told in twilight and darkness around fires for thousands of years. While they are entertaining and engaging stories in their own right, they are so in large part because they are emblematical of the dramas we encounter as we seek wholeness, happiness, and peace. The kings and queens, princes and princesses, dwarfs and witches, are not merely personages "out there." We know them intuitively as aspects of our own psyches, strands of our own being, groping toward fulfillment. We house the ogre *and* the witch, and they have to be faced and honored or they will consume us (eat us up). Fairy tales are ancient guidance, containing a wisdom, distilled through millennia of telling, for our instinctual survival, growth, and integration in the face of inner and outer demons and dragons, dark woods and wastelands. These stories remind us that it is worth seeking the altar where our own fragmented and isolated being-strands can find each other and marry, bringing new levels of harmony and understanding to our lives, to the point where we might actually live happily ever after, which really means in the timeless here and now. These stories are wise, ancient, surprisingly sophisticated blueprints for our full development as human beings.

One recurrent theme in the fairy stories is that of a young child, usually a prince or a princess, who loses his or her golden ball. Whether we ourselves are male or female, old or young, we each contain both prince and princess (among countless other figures), and there was a time we each radiated with the golden innocence and infinite promise carried by youth. And we still carry that golden radiance, or can recover it, if we take care not to let our development arrest.

Bly points out that between losing the golden ball, which seems to happen first around age eight, and taking any steps to recover it or even to recognize that it has gotten away from us, might take thirty or forty years, whereas in fairy tales, which take place "once upon a time," and therefore outside of ordinary time, usually it only takes a day or two. But in both instances a bargain needs to be made first, a bargain with our own suppressed shadow energies, symbolized by a frog or perhaps by a hairy wild man who resides under the pond in the forest, as in *Iron John*.

Before that bargain can be made, you have to know that these creatures are there, prince and princess, frog, wild man or wild woman. Conversing with those aspects of our psyches that we instinctively turn away from into unconsciousness is a prerequisite. And that may be plenty scary, because the feeling state that arises is the one that comes when we go down into dark, unknown, mysterious places.

The form of Buddhism that took root and flowered in Tibet from the eighth century until our day developed perhaps the most refined artistic expression of these terrifying aspects of the human psyche. Many Tibetan statues and paintings are of grotesque demonic beings, all respected members of the pantheon of honored deities. Keep in mind that these deities are not gods in the usual sense. Rather, they represent different mind states, each with its own kind of divine energy which has to be faced, honored, and worked with if we are to grow and develop our true potential as full human beings, whether men or women. These wrathful creatures are not seen as bad, even though their appearance is frightening and repulsive, with their necklaces of skulls and grotesque grimaces. Their terrible outward appearance is actually a disguise adopted by deities embodying wisdom and compassion to help us attain greater understanding and kindness toward ourselves and toward others, who, it is understood, are not fundamentally different from ourselves.

In Buddhism, the vehicle for this work of inner development is meditation. Even in the fairy tales, to get in touch with the wild man under the pond requires bucketing out the pond, something Bly points out takes repetitive inner work over a long time. There is nothing glamorous about bucketing out a pond, or working at a hot forge, or in the sweltering vineyards, day after day, year after year. But repetitive inner work of this kind, coming to know the forces of one's own psyche, is its own initiation. It is a tempering process. Usually heat is involved. It takes discipline to tolerate the heat, to persevere. But what comes of keeping at it is mastery and non-naivete, attainment of an inward order unattainable without the discipline, the heat, the descent into our darkness and fear. Even the interior defeats we suffer serve us in this tempering.

This is what Jungians call soul work, the development of depth of character through knowing something of the tortuous labyrinthine depths and expanses of our own minds. The heat tempers, rearranging the very atoms of our psychic being and, most likely, of our bodies as well.

The beauty of meditative work is that it is possible to rely on the practice itself to guide us through the maze. It keeps us on the path, even in the darkest of moments, facing the most terrifying of our own mind states and external circumstances. It reminds us of our options. It is a guide to human development, a roadmap to our radiant selves, not to the gold of a childhood innocence already past, but to that of a fully developed adult. But, for meditation to do its work, we have to be willing to do ours. We must be willing to encounter darkness and despair when they come up and face them, over and over again if need be, without running away or numbing ourselves in the thousands of ways we conjure up to avoid the unavoidable.

T R Y : Being open to the prince and the princess, the king and the queen, the giant and the witch, the wild man and the wild woman, the dwarf and the crone, and the warrior, the healer, and the trickster within yourself. When you meditate, put the welcome mat out to all of them. Try sitting like a king or queen, or a warrior, or a sage. In times of great turmoil or darkness, use your breath as the string which will guide you through the labyrinth. Keep mindfulness alive even in the darkest moments, reminding yourself that the awareness is not part of the darkness or the pain; it holds the pain, and knows it, so it has to be more fundamental, and closer to what is healthy and strong and golden within you.

Practice as a Path

In the middle of this road we call our life
I found myself in a dark wood
With no clear path through.

DANTE ALIGHIERI,
Divine Comedy, "Inferno"

The journey metaphor is used in all cultures to describe life and the quest for meaning. In the East, the word *Tao,* Chinese for "Way" or "Path," carries this meaning. In Buddhism, meditation practice is usually spoken of as a path—the path of mindfulness, the path of right understanding, the path of the wheel of truth (Dharma). *Tao* and *Dharma* also mean the way things are, the law that governs all of existence and non-existence. All events, whether we see them on the surface as good or bad, are fundamentally in harmony with the Tao. It is our job to learn to perceive this underlying harmony, and to live and make decisions in accord with it. Yet, frequently, it is not exactly clear what the right way is, which leaves plenty of room for free will and principled action, and also for tension and controversy, to say nothing of getting lost entirely.

When we practice meditation, we are really acknowledging

that in this moment, we are on the road of life. The path unfolds in this moment and in every moment while we are alive. Meditation is more rightly thought of as a "Way" than as a technique. It is a Way of being, a Way of living, a Way of listening, a Way of walking along the path of life and being in harmony with things as they are. This means in part acknowledging that sometimes, often at very crucial times, you really have no idea where you are going or even where the path lies. At the same time, you can very well know something about where you are now (even if it is knowing that you are lost, confused, enraged, or without hope). On the other hand, it often happens that we can become trapped into believing too strongly that we *do* know where we are going, especially if we are driven by self-serving ambition and we want certain things very badly. There is a blindness that comes from self-furthering agendas that leaves us thinking we know when actually we don't know as much as we think.

"The Water of Life," a fairy tale in the Grimm Brothers' collection, tells of the customary trio of brothers, princes all. The two oldest brothers are greedy and selfish. The youngest is kind and caring. Their father, the King, is dying. An old man who mysteriously appears in the palace garden inquires after their grief, and when he hears the problem, suggests that a cure might be had in the water of life. "If the King drinks of it, he will become well again; but it is hard to find."

First, the oldest brother obtains permission to go forth to seek the water of life for his father, harboring the secret hope of currying his favor and becoming King himself. Almost as soon as he sets out on his horse, he encounters a dwarf beside the road who stops him and asks where he is going so fast. In his hurry, the brother treats the dwarf with scorn and condescension, ordering him out of his way. The presumption here is that the prince knows the way just because he knows what he is looking for. Not so. But this brother is unable to rein in his arrogance, and his ignorance of the many ways things might unfold or open up in life.

Of course, the dwarf in fairy tales is no outer person either, but symbolic of the higher powers of the soul. In this case, the selfish brother is unable to approach his own inner power and feeling self with kindness and wisdom. Because of his arrogance, the dwarf arranges for his path to enter an ever-narrowing ravine, in which he eventually finds himself unable to go forward, unable to go back, and unable to turn around; in a word, stuck. And there he stays while the story continues.

When the first brother does not return, the second brother goes forth to try his luck, meets the dwarf, treats him in the same fashion, and winds up stuck just like the first brother. Since they are different parts of the same person, you might say some people never learn.

After some time, the third brother eventually sets off to bring back the water of life. He too encounters the dwarf, who asks where he is going in such a hurry. However, unlike his brothers, he stops, dismounts, and tells the dwarf of his father's grave illness and of seeking the water of life, admitting that he has no idea where to look or in what direction to go. At that, of course, the dwarf says, "Oh, I know where that is to be found," and he proceeds to tell him where it is and how he is to go about getting it, which is quite complicated. This brother listens carefully and remembers what he is told.

This richly crafted tale takes many turns in its unfolding, which I will leave to the interested reader to explore. The point here is simply that it is useful at times to admit to yourself that you don't know your way and to be open to help from unexpected places. Doing this makes available to you inner and outer energies and allies that arise out of your own soulfulness and selflessness. Of course, the selfish brothers are also internal figures of the psyche. The message is that getting caught up in the normal human tendencies of self-cherishing and arrogance, and ignoring the larger order of things, will ultimately lead to an impasse in your life in which you are unable to go forward, unable to go back, and unable to turn around. The story says you will never find the water of life with such an attitude, and that you will remain stuck, potentially forever.

The work of mindfulness demands honoring and heeding our own dwarf energy, rather than rushing headlong into things with a mind that is sorely out of touch with large parts of ourself, a mind driven by narrow ambition and ideas of personal gain. The story says we can only fare well if we proceed with an awareness of the way things are, including a willingness to admit not knowing where we are going. The youngest brother has a long road to travel in the story before it can be said that he fully understands the way things are (with his brothers, for instance). He endures painful lessons in treachery and betrayal, and he pays a high price for his naivete before finally owning the full range of his energy and wisdom. These are symbolized by his ultimately riding straight down the middle of a road paved in gold and marrying the princess (I haven't told you about her) and becoming King—a fully developed man, not of his father's kingdom but of his own.

T R Y : Seeing your own life this very day as a journey and as an adventure. Where are you going? What are you seeking? Where are you now? What stage of the journey have you come to? If your life were a book, what would you call it today? What would you entitle the chapter you are in right now? Are you stuck here in certain ways? Can you be fully open to all of the energies at your disposal at this point? Note that this journey is uniquely yours, no one else's. So the path has to be your own.

You cannot imitate somebody else's journey and still be true to yourself. Are you prepared to honor your uniqueness in this way? Can you see a commitment to the meditation practice as an intimate part of this way of being? Can you commit to lighting your path with mindfulness and awareness? Can you see ways in which you could easily get stuck, or have in the past?

Meditation: Not to Be Confused with Positive Thinking

Our ability to think the way we do differentiates our species from all others and is miraculous beyond compare. But if we are not careful, our thinking can easily crowd out other equally precious and miraculous facets of our being. Wakefulness is often the first casualty.

Awareness is not the same as thought. It lies beyond thinking, although it makes use of thinking, honoring its value and its power. Awareness is more like a vessel which can hold and contain our thinking, helping us to see and know our thoughts as thoughts rather than getting caught up in them as reality.

The thinking mind can at times be severely fragmented. In fact, it almost always is. This is the nature of thought. But awareness, teased out of each moment with conscious intent, can help us to perceive that even in the midst of this fragmentation, our fundamental nature is already integrated and whole. Not only is it not limited by the potpourri of our thinking mind, awareness is the pot which cradles all the fragments, just as the soup pot holds all the chopped-up carrots, peas, onions, and the like and allows them to cook into one whole, the soup itself. But it is a magical pot, much like a sorcerer's pot, because it cooks things without having to do anything, even put a fire underneath it. Awareness itself does the cooking, as long as it is sustained. You just let the fragments stir while you hold them in awareness. Whatever comes up in mind or body goes into the pot, becomes part of the soup.

Meditation does not involve trying to change your thinking by thinking some more. It involves watching thought itself. The watching is the holding. By watching your thoughts without being drawn into them, you can learn something profoundly liberating about thinking itself, which may help you to be less of a prisoner of those thought patterns—often so strong in us—which are narrow, inaccurate, self-involved, habitual to the point of being imprisoning, and also just plain wrong.

Another way to look at meditation is to view the process of thinking itself as a waterfall, a continual cascading of thought. In cultivating mindfulness, we are going *beyond* or *behind* our thinking, much the way you might find a vantagepoint in a cave or depression in the rock behind a waterfall. We still see and hear the water, but we are out of the torrent.

Practicing in this way, our thought patterns change by themselves in ways that nourish integration, understanding, and compassion in our lives, but *not* because we are trying to make them change by replacing one thought with another one that we think may be more pure. Rather, it is to understand the nature of our thoughts *as thoughts* and our relationship to them, so that they can be more at our service rather than the other way round.

If we decide to think positively, that may be useful, but it is not meditation. It is just more thinking. We can as easily become a prisoner of so-called positive thinking as of negative thinking. It too can be confining, fragmented, inaccurate, illusory, self-serving, and wrong. Another element altogether is required to induce transformation in our lives and take us beyond the limits of thought.

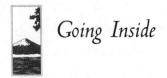

Going Inside

It is easy to come by the impression that meditation is about going inside, or dwelling inside yourself. But "inside" and "outside" are limited distinctions. In the stillness of formal practice, we do turn our energies inward, only to discover that we contain the entire world in our own mind and body.

Dwelling inwardly for extended periods, we come to know something of the poverty of always looking outside ourselves for happiness, understanding, and wisdom. It's not that God, the environment, and other people cannot help us to be happy or to find satisfaction. It's just that our happiness, satisfaction, and our understanding, even of God, will be no deeper than our capacity to know ourselves inwardly, to encounter the outer world from the deep comfort that comes from being at home in one's own skin, from an intimate familiarity with the ways of one's own mind and body.

Dwelling in stillness and looking inward for some part of each day, we touch what is most real and reliable in ourselves and most easily overlooked and undeveloped. When we can be centered in ourselves, even for brief periods of time in the face of the pull of the outer world, not having to look elsewhere for something to fill us up or make us happy, we can be at home wherever we find ourselves, at peace with things as they are, moment by moment.

*

Don't go outside your house to see the flowers.
My friend, don't bother with that excursion.
Inside your body there are flowers.
One flower has a thousand petals.
That will do for a place to sit.
Sitting there you will have a glimpse of beauty
inside the body and out of it,
before gardens and after gardens.

KABIR

*

The heavy is the root of the light.
The unmoved is the source of all movement.

Thus the Master travels all day
without leaving home.
However splendid the views,
she stays serenely in herself.

Why should the lord of the country
flit about like a fool?
If you let yourself be blown to and fro,
you lose touch with your root.
If you let restlessness move you,
you lose touch with who you are.

LAO-TZU, *Tao-te-Ching*

*

Direct your eye right inward, and you'll find
A thousand regions in your mind
Yet undiscovered. Travel them and be
Expert in home-cosmography.

THOREAU, *Walden*

TRY: The next time you feel a sense of dissatisfaction, of something being missing or not quite right, turn inward just as an experiment. See if you can capture the energy of that very moment. Instead of picking up a magazine or going to the movies, calling a friend or looking for something to eat or acting up in one way or another, make a place for yourself. Sit down and enter into your breathing, if only for a few minutes. Don't look for anything—neither flowers nor light nor a beautiful view. Don't extol the virtues of anything or condemn the inadequacy of anything. Don't even think to yourself, "I am going inward now." Just sit. Reside at the center of the world. Let things be as they are.

Part Two

The Heart of Practice

What lies behind us and what lies before us are
tiny matters compared to what lies within us.

OLIVER WENDELL HOLMES

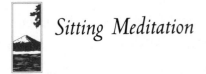

Sitting Meditation

What is so special about sitting? Nothing, when we speak of the way we ordinarily sit. It's just one convenient way our bodies take a load off our feet. But sitting is very special when it comes to meditation.

You can know that superficially easily enough from the outside. For instance, you might not know that a person is meditating when you see him standing or lying down, or walking, but you know it immediately when he is sitting, especially if he is sitting on the floor. From any angle, the posture itself embodies wakefulness, even when the eyes are closed and the face is serene and peaceful. It is mountainlike in its majesty and solidity. There is a stability to it which speaks volumes, broadcasting inwardly and outwardly. The moment the person dozes off, all these qualities evaporate. The mind collapses inwardly, the body visibly.

Sitting meditation involves sitting in an upright, dignified posture, often for extended periods of time. While it is relatively easy to assume an erect posture, that is just the beginning of this challenging process of continual unfolding. You may readily enough "park" your body, but there is still the question of what the mind is up to. Sitting meditation is not a matter of taking on a special body posture, however powerful that may be. It is adopting a particular posture toward the mind. It is mind sitting.

Once you are sitting, there are many ways to approach the present moment. All involve paying attention on purpose, non-judgmentally. What varies is what you attend to and how.

It is best to keep things simple and start with your breathing, feeling it as it moves in and out. Ultimately, you can expand your awareness to observe all the comings and goings, the gyrations and machinations of your own thoughts and feelings, perceptions and impulses, body and mind. But it may take some time for concentration and mindfulness to become strong enough to hold such a wide range of objects in awareness without getting lost in them or attached to particular ones, or simply overwhelmed. For most of us, it takes years and depends a good deal on your motivation and the intensity of your practice. So, at the beginning, you might want to stay with the breath, or use it as an anchor to bring you back when you are carried away. Try it for a few years and see what happens.

TRY: Setting aside a time every day for just being. Five minutes would be fine, or ten or twenty or thirty if you want to venture that far. Sit down and watch the moments unfold, with no agenda other than to be fully present. Use the breath as an anchor to tether your attention to the present moment. Your thinking mind will drift here and there, depending on the currents and winds moving in the mind until, at some point, the anchorline grows taut and brings you back. This may happen a lot. Bring your attention back to the breath, in all its vividness, every time it wanders. Keep the posture erect but not stiff. Think of yourself as a mountain.

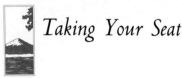

Taking Your Seat

It helps to come to the cushion or to the chair with a definite sense of *taking your seat.* Sitting meditation is different from just sitting down casually somewhere. There is energy in the statement the sitting makes as you take your seat, both in the choice of spot, and in mindfulness filling your body. The posture embodies a *stand,* as in "taking a stand," even though you are sitting. There is a strong sense of honoring place and placement of body and mind and moment.

We take our seat to meditate keeping all this in mind, yet without any investment in location or posture. There may indeed be definite "power spots" indoors and out, yet with this attitude of taking a stand, you can sit anywhere in any posture and be at home. When your mind and body collaborate in holding body, time, place, and posture in awareness, and remain unattached to having it have to be a certain way, then and only then are you truly sitting.

Dignity

When we describe the sitting posture, the word that feels the most appropriate is "dignity."

Sitting down to meditate, our posture talks to us. It makes its own statement. You might say the posture itself is the meditation. If we slump, it reflects low energy, passivity, a lack of clarity. If we sit ramrod-straight, we are tense, making too much of an effort, trying too hard. When I use the word "dignity" in teaching situations, as in "Sit in a way that embodies dignity," everybody immediately adjusts their posture to sit up straighter. But they don't stiffen. Faces relax, shoulders drop, head, neck, and back come into easy alignment. The spine rises out of the pelvis with energy. Sometimes people tend to sit forward, away from the backs of their chairs, more autonomously. Everybody seems to instantly know that inner feeling of dignity and how to embody it.

Perhaps we just need little reminders from time to time that we are already dignified, deserving, worthy. Sometimes we don't feel that way because of the wounds and the scars we carry from the past or because of the uncertainty of the future. It is doubtful that we came to feel undeserving on our own. We were helped to feel unworthy. We were taught it in a thousand ways when we were little, and we learned our lessons well.

So, when we take our seat in meditation and remind ourselves to sit with dignity, we are coming back to our original worthiness. That in itself is quite a statement. You can bet our inside will be listening. Are we ready to listen, too? Are we ready to listen to the currents of direct experience in this moment, and this one, and this . . . ?

T R Y : Sitting with dignity for thirty seconds. Note how you feel. Try it standing with dignity. Where are your shoulders? How is your spine, your head? What would it mean to walk with dignity?

Posture

When you sit with strong intentionality, the body itself makes a statement of deep conviction and commitment in its carriage. These radiate inward and outward. A dignified sitting posture is itself an affirmation of freedom, and of life's harmony, beauty, and richness.

Sometimes you feel in touch with it; other times you may not. Even when you feel depressed, burdened, confused, sitting can affirm the strength and value of this life lived now. If you can muster the patience to sustain your sitting for even a brief time, it can bring you in touch with the very core of your being, that domain which is beyond up or down, free or burdened, clear-sighted or confused. This core is akin to awareness itself; it doesn't fluctuate with mental state or life circumstances. It is mirrorlike, impartially reflecting what comes before it. This includes a deep knowing that whatever is present, whatever has happened to shake your life or overwhelm you, will of itself inevitably change, and for this reason alone, bears simply hold-ing in the mirror of the present moment—watching it, embrac-ing its presence, riding its waves of unfolding just as you ride the waves of your own breathing, and having faith that you will sooner or later find a way to act, to come to terms, to move through and beyond. Not by trying so much as by watching, by letting things be, and feeling them fully moment by moment.

Mindful sitting meditation is not an attempt to escape from problems or difficulties into some cut-off "meditative" state of absorption or denial. On the contrary, it is a willingness to go nose to nose with pain, confusion, and loss, if that is what is dominating the present moment, and to stay with the observing over a sustained period of time, beyond thinking. You seek understanding simply through bearing the situation in mind, along with your breath, as you maintain the sitting posture.

In the Zen tradition, one teacher (Shunru Suzuki Roshi) put it this way: "The state of mind that exists when you sit in the right posture is itself enlightenment. . . . These forms [sitting meditation] are not the means of obtaining the right state of mind. To take this posture is itself the right state of mind." In the sitting meditation, you are already touching your own truest nature.

So, when we practice sitting meditation, first and foremost it means sitting in such a way that your body affirms, radiates, broadcasts an attitude of presence, that you are committed to acknowledging and accepting whatever comes up in any moment. This orientation is one of non-attachment and unwavering stability, like a clear mirror, only reflecting, itself empty, receptive, open. This attitude is contained in the posture, in the very way you choose to sit. The posture embodies the attitude.

This is why many people find the image of a mountain

positions. In the case of sitting meditation, sometimes the hands are on the knees, palms down; sometimes one or both palms are up; sometimes one or more fingers of one hand are touching the ground, while the other hand is raised up. Sometimes the hands are together in the lap, with the fingers of one hand lying atop the fingers of the other, the thumbtips gently touching as if circling an invisible egg to form what is called the "cosmic mudra." Sometimes the fingers and palms are placed together over the heart in the traditional posture of Christian prayer. This same posture, in Oriental greeting, signifies a bow in recognition of the divinity within the other person.

These hand mudras all embody different energies, which you can experiment with yourself in meditation. Try sitting with your hands palms down on your knees. Notice the quality of self-containment here. To me, this posture speaks of not looking for anything more, but simply digesting what is.

If you then turn both palms up, being mindful as you do it, you may note a change in energy in the body. To me, sitting this way embodies receptivity, an openness to what is above, to the energy of the heavens (the Chinese say: "As above, so below"). Sometimes I feel a strong impulse to open to energy from above. It can be quite helpful at times, especially in periods of turmoil or confusion, to emphasize receptivity in your sitting practice. This can be done simply by opening your palms to the heavens. It's not that you are actively looking for something to magically help you. Rather, you are making yourself available to higher insights, priming a willingness in yourself to resonate with energies we usually think of as elevated, divine, celestial, cosmic, universal, of a higher order and wisdom.

All our hand postures are mudras in that they are associated with subtle or not-so-subtle energies. Take the energy of the fist, for instance. When we get angry, our hands tend to close into fists. Some people unknowingly practice this mudra a lot in their lives. It waters the seeds of anger and violence within you every time you do it, and they respond by sprouting and growing stronger.

The next time you find yourself making fists out of anger, try to bring mindfulness to the inner attitude embodied in a fist. Feel the tension, the hatred, the anger, the aggression, and the fear which it contains. Then, in the midst of your anger, as an experiment, if the person you are angry at is present, try opening your fists and placing the palms together over your heart in the prayer position right in front of him. (Of course, he won't have the slightest idea what you are doing.) Notice what happens to the anger and hurt as you hold this position for even a few moments.

I find it virtually impossible to sustain my anger when I do this. It's not that the anger may not be justified. It's just that all sorts of other feelings come into play, which frame the anger energy and tame it—feelings like sympathy and compassion for the other person, and perhaps a greater understanding of the dance we are both in . . . The dance of one thing inevitably

leading to another, of the concatenation of consequences impersonally set in motion, the end result of which can (mistakenly)
be taken personally and lead to ignorance compounding ignorance, aggression compounding aggression, with no wisdom
anywhere.

When Gandhi was assassinated at pointblank range, he put
his palms together in this way toward his attacker, uttered his
mantra, and died. Years of meditation and yoga practice, guided
by his beloved Bhagavad Gita, had brought him to the point
where he was able to bring the perspective of non-attachment to
everything he was engaged in, including his very life. It allowed
him to choose the attitude he would take in that very moment
he was being robbed of life. He didn't die angry or even
surprised. He had known his life was in constant danger. But
he had trained himself to march to the drumbeat of his own
growing vision of what constituted wise action. He had come to
a point where he truly embodied compassion. He lived an
unwavering commitment to both political and spiritual freedom. His personal well-being was of limited value in comparison. He was always putting it on the line.

TRY: Being aware of subtle emotional qualities you may be embodying at various times of the day, as well as during your sitting practice. Pay particular attention to your hands. Does their position make a difference? See if you don't become more mindful by becoming more "bodyful."

As you practice being more in touch with your hands in sitting meditation, see if this doesn't have an influence on the way you touch. Everything from opening a door to making love involves touch. It is possible to open a door so mindlessly that your hand doesn't know what your body is doing and you hit yourself in the head with it. Imagine the challenge of touching another person without automaticity, with no gaining idea, just presence and caring.

Coming Out of Meditation

The moments toward the end of a period of formal meditation have their own tricky topology. Mindfulness can become lax with the anticipation of finishing. How you handle this is important. It is precisely such transitions that challenge us to deepen our mindfulness and extend its range.

Toward the end of a period of formal practice, if you are not particularly attentive, before you know it you'll be off doing something else, with no awareness whatsoever of how the meditation came to an end. The transition will be a blur at best. You can bring mindfulness to this process by being in touch with the thoughts and impulses which tell you it's time to stop. Whether you've been still for an hour or for three minutes, a powerful feeling all of a sudden may say, "This is enough." Or you look at your watch and it's the time you said you would quit.

In your meditation practice, especially when you are not using a tape for guidance, see if you can detect the very first impulse to quit, and any others that may follow, growing in strength. As you recognize each impulse, breathe with it for a few moments, and ask yourself, "Who has had enough?" Try looking into what is behind the impulse. Is it fatigue, boredom, pain, impatience; or is it just time to stop? Whatever the case, rather than automatically leaping up or moving on, try lingering with whatever arises out of this inquiry, breathing with it for a few moments or even longer, and allowing the moving out of your meditation posture to be as much an object of moment-to-moment awareness as any other moment in the meditation.

Practicing like this can increase mindfulness in many different situations that involve closing or ending something and moving on to something else. It can be as simple and brief as being in touch with closing a door, or as complicated and painful as when an era in your life comes to an end. So much automaticity can creep into closing a door, because it's so unimportant in the overall scheme of things (unless the baby is sleeping). But it is precisely because it is relatively unimportant that closing the door mindfully activates and deepens our sensitivity, our capacity to be in touch with all of our moments, and smooths out some of the deeper wrinkles of our habitual unconsciousness.

Curiously, just as much if not more mindless behavior can creep into our most momentous closures and life transitions, including our own aging and our own dying. Here, too, mindfulness can have healing effects. We may be so defended against feeling the full impact of our emotional pain—whether it be grief, sadness, shame, disappointment, anger, or for that matter, even joy or satisfaction—that we unconsciously escape into a cloud of numbness in which we do not permit ourselves to feel anything at all or know what we are feeling. Like a fog, unawareness blankets precisely those moments that might be the most profound occasions to see impermanence at work, to be in touch with the universal and impersonal aspects of being and becoming that underlie our personalized emotional investments, to touch the mystery of being small, fragile, and temporary, and to come to peace with the absolute inevitability of change.

In the Zen tradition, group sitting meditations are sometimes ended with a loud wooden clacker which is whacked together forcefully. No romantic lingering with the sound of a soft bell to ease the end of a sitting. The message here is to cut—time to move on now. If you're daydreaming, even slightly, when the clacker goes off, the sound will startle you and thereby point out how little you were actually present in that moment. It reminds you that the sitting is already over and now we are in a new moment, to be faced anew.

In other traditions, the gentle ring of a bell is used to mark the end of group sittings. The softness of the bell brings you back too, and also points out whether your mind was on the loose at the moment it rang. So, when it comes to ending a sitting, soft and gentle is good, and hard and loud is good. Both remind us to be fully present in moments of transition, that all endings are also beginnings, that what is most important, in the words of the Diamond Sutra, is to "develop a mind that clings to nothing." Only then will we be able to see things as they actually are and respond with the full range of our emotional capacity and our wisdom.

*

The Master sees things as they are,
without trying to control them.
She lets them go their own way,
and resides at the center of the circle.

LAO-TZU, *Tao-te-Ching*

TRY: Bringing awareness to how you end your meditations. Whether they are lying down, sitting, standing, or walking, zero in on "who" ends it, how it ends, when it ends, and why. Don't judge it or yourself in any way—just observe, and stay in touch with the transition from one thing to the next.

How Long to Practice?

Q: Dr. Kabat-Zinn, how long should I meditate?
A: How should I know?

It keeps coming up, this question of how long to meditate. We felt from the beginning of our work using meditation with patients in the hospital that it would be important for them to be exposed right from the start to relatively extended periods of practice. Since we believed strongly in the principle that if you ask a lot of people or ask them to ask a lot of themselves, then you will get a lot, whereas if you ask only a little, the most you are likely to get is a little, we went with forty-five minutes as the basic required practice time at home every day. Forty-five minutes seemed long enough to settle into stillness and sustained attending from moment to moment, and perhaps to experience at least tastes of a deepening relaxation and sense of well-being. It also seemed long enough to allow for ample opportunity to engage the more challenging mind states that we ordinarily hope to avoid because they take over our lives and severely tax (when they don't overwhelm completely) our ability to remain calm and mindful. The usual suspects, of course, are boredom, impatience, frustration, fear, anxiety (which would include worrying about all the things you might be accomplishing if you weren't wasting time meditating), fantasy, memories, anger, pain, fatigue, and grief.

It turned out to be a good intuition. Most of the people coming through our clinic have willingly made the almost never easy adjustments in the day-to-day conduct of their lives to practice daily for forty-five minutes at a stretch, at least over a period of eight weeks. And many never stray from that new life path. It not only becomes easy, it becomes necessary, a lifeline.

But there is a flip side to this way of looking at things. What may be challenging but doable for one person at one time in her or his life may be nigh impossible at another time even for that same person. Perceptions of "long" and "short" are at best relative. The single mother of small children is unlikely to have forty-five minutes at a stretch for anything. Does that mean she can't meditate?

If your life is in perpetual crisis, or you find yourself immersed in social and economic chaos, you may have trouble finding the psychic energy to meditate for extended periods, even if you have the time. Something always seems to come up to get in the way, especially if you are thinking you have to have a forty-five-minute clearing in your day even to get started. Practicing in cramped quarters around the lives of other family members can make for uncomfortable feelings which may become obstacles to daily practice.

Medical students can hardly be expected routinely to carve

out extended periods for non-doing, nor can many other people in high-stress jobs and demanding situations. Nor can folks who are just curious about meditation but have no strong reason to push the limits of convenience and of their own sense of time pressure or comfort.

For those seeking balance in their lives, a certain flexibility of approach is not only helpful, it is essential. It is important to know that meditation has little to do with clock time. Five minutes of formal practice can be as profound or more so than forty-five minutes. The sincerity of your effort matters far more than elapsed time, since we are really talking about stepping out of minutes and hours and into moments, which are truly dimensionless and therefore infinite. So, if you have some motivation to practice even a little, that is what is important. Mindfulness needs to be kindled and nurtured, protected from the winds of a busy life or a restless and tormented mind, just as a small flame needs to be sheltered from strong gusts of air.

If you can only manage five minutes, or even one minute of mindfulness at first, that is truly wonderful. It means you have already remembered the value of stopping, of shifting even momentarily from doing to being.

When we teach meditation to medical students to help them with the stress and sometimes the trauma of medical education in its present form, or to college athletes who want to train their minds along with their bodies to optimize performance, or to people in a pulmonary rehabilitation program who need to learn a lot of other things as well as meditate, or to employees in a lunchtime stress reduction class, we don't insist on forty-five minutes of practice a day. (We only do that with our own patients, or with people who are ready to make such an intense lifestyle change for reasons of their own.) Instead, we challenge them to practice every day for fifteen minutes at a time, or twice a day if they can manage that.

If you think about it for a moment, few of us—no matter what we do or what situation we find ourselves in—would be unable to free up one or two fifteen-minute blocks of time out of twenty-four hours. And if not fifteen, then ten, or five.

Recall that in a line six inches long, there are an infinite number of points, and in a line one inch long there are just as many. Well, then, how many moments are there in fifteen minutes, or five, or ten, or forty-five? It turns out we have plenty of time, if we are willing to hold any moments at all in awareness.

Forming the intention to practice and then seizing a moment—any moment—and encountering it fully in your inward and outward posture, lies at the core of mindfulness. Long and short periods of practice are both good, but "long" may never flourish if your frustration and the obstacles in your path loom too large. Far better to adventure into longer periods of practice gradually on your own than never to taste mindfulness or stillness because the perceived obstacles were too great. A journey of a thousand miles really does begin with a single step. When we commit to taking that step—in this case, to taking our seat for even the briefest of times—we can touch the timeless in any moment. From that all benefit flows, and from that alone.

*

When you really look for me, you will see me instantly— you will find me in the tiniest house of time.

KABIR

T R Y : Sitting for varying lengths of clock time. See how it affects your practice. Does your concentration lapse as you sit longer? Do you get hung up in how much longer you "have" to be present? Does impatience come up at some point? Does the mind get reactive or obsessive? Is there restlessness? Anxiety? Boredom? Time pressure? Sleepiness? Dullness? If you are new to meditation, are you finding yourself saying, "This is stupid," or, "Am I doing it right?", or, "Is this all I am supposed to be feeling?"

Do these feelings start right away or do they only come up after a while? Can you see them as mind states? Can you observe them without judging them or yourself for even brief periods? If you put the welcome mat out for them and investigate their qualities and let them be, you may learn a lot about what is strong and unwavering in yourself. And what is strong in you may become even stronger as you nourish inner stability and calmness.

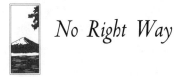

No Right Way

Backpacking with my family in Teton wilderness, I am recurrently struck by the question of footing. With each step, the foot has to come down somewhere. Climbing or descending over boulder fields, steep inclines, on and off trails, our feet make split-second decisions for us about where and how to come down, what angle, how much pressure, heel or toe, rotated or straight. The kids don't ever ask: "Daddy, where do I put my feet? Should I step on this rock or that one?" They just do it, and I've noticed that they find a way—they choose where to put their feet at each step, and it's not simply where I put mine.

What this says to me is that our feet find their own way. Watching my own, I am amazed at how many different places and ways I might put my foot down with each step, and how out of this unfolding momentary potential, the foot ultimately commits to one way, executes with full weight on it (or less if it's a hazardous situation), and then lets go as the next foot makes its choice and I move forward. All this occurs virtually without thinking, except at the occasional tricky spots where thought and experience do come into play and I might have to give my youngest child, Serena, a hand. But that is the exception, not the rule. Ordinarily we are not looking at our feet and thinking about each step. We are looking out, ahead on the trail, and our brain, taking it all in, makes split-second decisions for us that put the foot down in a way that conforms to the needs of the terrain underfoot in that moment.

This doesn't mean that there is no wrong way to step. You do have to be careful and sense your footing. It's just that the eyes and the brain are very good at rapid assessment of terrain and giving detailed directions to torso, limbs, and feet, so that the whole process of taking a step on rough ground is one of exquisite balance in motion, even with the complication of boots and heavy packs. There is built-in mindfulness here. Rough terrain brings it out in us. And if we do a trail ten times, we'll each solve the problem of each footstep differently each time. Covering ground on foot always unfolds out of the uniqueness of the present moment.

It's no different in meditation. There is really and truly no one "right way" to practice, although there are pitfalls along this path too and they have to be looked out for. It is best to encounter each moment with freshness, its rich potential held in awareness. We look deeply into it, and then we let go into the next moment, not holding to the last one. Each moment then can be fresh, each breath a new beginning, a new letting go, a new letting be. Just as with our stepping over rocky terrain, there is no "supposed to" here. True, there is much to be seen and understood along this path; but it can't be forced, any more than you can force someone to appreciate the golden light of the low sun shining over fields of wheat or the moonrise in the mountains. Best not to speak at all in moments such as these. All you can do is be present with the enormity of it yourself and hope others see it in the silence of the moment. Sunsets and moonrises speak for themselves, in their own languages, on their own canvases. Silence at times leaves space for the untamed to speak.

In the same way, in the meditation practice, it is best to hold to and honor one's own direct experience, and not worry too much about whether *this* is what you are supposed to feel or see or think about. Why not trust your experience in this moment just as you would trust your foot to find a way to keep you balanced as you move over rocks? If you practice this kind of trust in the face of insecurity and the strong habit of wanting some authority to anoint your experience (however minuscule, and it usually is) with his/her blessing, you will find that something of a deepening nature does happen along the path. Our feet and our breath both teach us to watch our step, to proceed mindfully, to truly be at home in every moment, wherever our feet carry us, to appreciate where we are. What greater gift could be bestowed upon us?

TRY: Being aware of all the times in meditation when the thought comes up: "Am I doing this right?" "Is this what I should be feeling?" "Is this what is 'supposed' to happen?" Instead of trying to answer these questions, just look more deeply into the present moment. Expand your awareness in this very moment. Hold the question in awareness along with your breathing and with the full range of this particular moment's context. Trust that in this moment, "This is it," whatever and wherever "this" is. Looking deeply into whatever the "this" of the present moment is, keep up a continuity of mindfulness, allowing one moment to unfold into the next without analyzing, discoursing, judging, condemning, or doubting; simply observing, embracing, opening, letting be, accepting. Right now. Only this step. Only this moment.

A What-Is-My-Way? Meditation

We are quick to tell our children that they can't always have their own way, even implying that there is something wrong with wanting it. And when they ask, "Why not, Mommy?", "Why not, Daddy?", and we have come to the end of our explanations or our patience, we are likely to say, "Never mind. Just listen to me. You'll understand when you grow up."

But isn't this more than a little unfair? Don't we adults behave in exactly the same way as our children? Don't we want to have things our own way too, all the time if possible? How are we different from the children except that we are less honest and open about it? And what if we *could* have our own way? What would it be? Do you remember the trouble that people get into in fairy tales when they are offered three wishes by a genie or a dwarf or a witch?

The people of Maine are known for saying, "You can't get there from here," when asked for directions. In terms of life directions, perhaps it is truer to say, "You can only get there if you are fully here." How many of us are aware of this little twist in the fabric of fate?

Would we know what our way is if we could have it? Would getting our way solve anything at all, or would it only make more of a mess of our lives were it possible to realize our wishes on impulse out of our so frequently mindless states of mind?

The truly interesting question here is, "What exactly *is* my way?", meaning my "Way" with a capital W. Rarely do we contemplate our life with this degree of probing. How frequently do we linger in such basic questions as "Who am I?", "Where am I going?", "What path am I on?", "Is this the right direction for me?", "If I could choose a path now, in which direction would I head?", "What is my yearning, my path?", "What do I truly love?"

Contemplating "What is my Way?" is an excellent element to inject into our meditation practice. We don't have to come up with answers, nor think that there has to be one particular answer. Better not to think at all. Instead, only persist in asking the question, letting any answers that formulate just come of themselves and go of themselves. As with everything else in the meditation practice, we just watch, listen, note, let be, let go, and keep generating the question, "What is my Way?", "What is my path?", "Who am I?"

The intention here is to remain open to *not knowing*, perhaps allowing yourself to come to the point of admitting, "I don't know," and then experimenting with relaxing a bit into this not knowing instead of condemning yourself for it. After all, in this moment, it may be an accurate statement of how things are for you.

Inquiry of this kind itself leads to openings, to new understandings and visions and actions. Inquiry takes on a life of its own after a while. It permeates the pores of your being and breathes new vitality, vibrancy, and grace into the bland, the humdrum, the routine. Inquiry will wind up "doing you" rather than you doing it. This is a good way to find the path that lies closest to your heart. After all, the journey is one of heroic proportions, but so much more so if enlivened by wakefulness and a commitment to adventurous inquiry. As a human being, you are the central figure in the universal hero's mythic journey, the fairy tale, the Arthurian quest. For men and women alike, this journey is the trajectory between birth and death, a human life lived. No one escapes the adventure. We only work with it differently.

Can we be in touch with our own life unfolding? Can we rise to the occasion of our own humanity? Can we take on the challenges we meet, even seeking them out to test ourselves, to grow, to act in a principled way, to be true to ourselves, to find our own way, and ultimately not only have it but, more importantly, live it?

The Mountain Meditation

When it comes to meditation, mountains have a lot to teach, having archetypal significance in all cultures. Mountains are sacred places. People have always sought spiritual guidance and renewal in and among them. The mountain is the symbol of the prime axis of the world (Mt. Meru), the dwelling place of the gods (Mt. Olympus), the place the spiritual leader encounters God and receives his (her) commandments and covenant (Mt. Sinai). Mountains are held sacred, embodying dread and harmony, harshness and majesty. Rising above all else on our planet, they beckon and overwhelm with their sheer presence. Their nature is elemental, rock. Rock-hard. Rock-solid. Mountains are the place of visions, where one can touch the panoramic scale of the natural world and its intersection with life's fragile but tenacious rootings. Mountains have played key roles in our history and prehistory. To traditional peoples, mountains were and still are mother, father, guardian, protector, ally.

In meditation practice, it can be helpful sometimes to "borrow" these wonderful archetypal qualities of mountains and use them to bolster our intentionality and resolve to hold the moment with an elemental purity and simplicity. The mountain image held in the mind's eye and in the body can freshen our memory of why we are sitting in the first place, and of what it truly means, each time we take our seat, to dwell in the realm of non-doing. Mountains are quintessentially emblematic of abiding presence and stillness.

The mountain meditation can be practiced in the following way, or modified to resonate with your personal vision of the mountain and its meaning. It can be done in any posture, but I find it most powerful when I am sitting cross-legged on the floor, so that my body looks and feels most mountainlike, inside and out. Being in the mountains or in sight of a mountain is helpful but not at all necessary. It is the inner image which is the source of power here.

Picture the most beautiful mountain you know or know of or can imagine, one whose form speaks personally to you. As you focus on the image or the feeling of the mountain in your mind's eye, notice its overall shape, the lofty peak, the base rooted in the rock of the earth's crust, the steep or gently sloping sides. Note as well how massive it is, how unmoving, how beautiful whether seen from afar or up close—a beauty emanating from its unique signature of shape and form, and at the same time embodying universal qualities of "mountainness" transcending particular shape and form.

Perhaps your mountain has snow at the top and trees on the lower slopes. Perhaps it has one prominent peak, perhaps a series of peaks or a high plateau. However it appears, just sit and breathe with the image of this mountain, observing it, noting its qualities. When you feel ready, see if you can bring the mountain into your own body so that your body sitting here and the mountain of the mind's eye become one. Your head becomes the lofty peak; your shoulders and arms the sides of the mountain; your buttocks and legs the solid base rooted to your cushion on the floor or to your chair. Experience in your body the sense of uplift, the axial, elevated quality of the mountain deep in your own spine. Invite yourself to become a breathing mountain, unwavering in your stillness, completely what you are—beyond words and thought, a centered, rooted, unmoving presence.

Now, as well you know, throughout the day as the sun travels the sky, the mountain just sits. Light and shadow and colors are changing virtually moment to moment in the mountain's adamantine stillness. Even the untrained eye can see changes by the hour. These evoke those masterpieces of Claude Monet, who had the genius to set up many easels and paint the life of his inanimate subjects hour by hour, moving from canvas to canvas as the play of light, shadow, and color transformed cathedral, river, or mountain, and thereby wake up the viewer's eye. As the light changes, as night follows day and day night, the mountain just sits, simply being itself. It remains still as the seasons flow into one another and as the weather changes moment by moment and day by day. Calmness abiding all change.

In summer, there is no snow on the mountain, except perhaps for the very top or in crags shielded from direct sunlight. In the fall, the mountain may display a coat of brilliant fire colors; in winter, a blanket of snow and ice. In any season, it may at times find itself enshrouded in clouds or fog, or pelted by freezing rain. The tourists who come to visit may be disappointed if they can't see the mountain clearly, but it's all the same to the mountain—seen or unseen, in sun or clouds, broiling or frigid, it just sits, being itself. At times visited by violent storms, buffeted by snow and rain and winds of unthinkable magnitude, through it all the mountain sits. Spring comes, the birds sing in the trees once again, leaves return to the trees which lost them, flowers bloom in the high meadows and on the slopes, streams overflow with waters of melting snow. Through it all, the mountain continues to sit, unmoved by the weather, by what happens on the surface, by the world of appearances.

As we sit holding this image in our mind, we can embody the same unwavering stillness and rootedness in the face of everything that changes in our own lives over seconds, hours, and years. In our lives and in our meditation practice, we experience constantly the changing nature of mind and body and of the outer world. We experience periods of light and dark, vivid color and drab dullness. We experience storms of varying intensity and violence, in the outer world and in our own lives and minds. Buffeted by high winds, by cold and rain, we endure periods of darkness and pain as well as savoring moments of joy and uplift. Even our appearance changes constantly, just like the mountain's, experiencing a weather and a weathering of its own.

By becoming the mountain in our meditation, we can link up

with its strength and stability, and adopt them for our own. We can use its energies to support our efforts to encounter each moment with mindfulness, equanimity, and clarity. It may help us to see that our thoughts and feelings, our preoccupations, our emotional storms and crises, even the things that happen *to* us are much like the weather on the mountain. We tend to take it personally, but its strongest characteristic is impersonal. The weather of our own lives is not to be ignored or denied. It is to be encountered, honored, felt, known for what it is, and held in high awareness since it can kill us. In holding it in this way, we come to know a deeper silence and stillness and wisdom than we may have thought possible, right within the storms. Mountains have this to teach us, and more, if we can come to listen.

Yet, when all is said and done, the mountain meditation is only a device, a finger pointing us toward somewhere. We still have to look, then go. While the mountain image can help us become more stable, human beings are far more interesting and complex than mountains. We are breathing, moving, dancing mountains. We can be simultaneously hard like rock, firm, unmoving, and at the same time soft and gentle and flowing. We have a vast range of potential at our disposal. We can see and feel. We can know and understand. We can learn; we can grow; we can heal; especially if we learn to listen to the inner harmony of things and hold the central mountain axis through thick and thin.

*

The birds have vanished into the sky,
and now the last cloud drains away.

We sit together, the mountain and me,
until only the mountain remains.

LI PO

TRY: Keeping this mountain image in mind as you sit in formal meditation. Explore its usefulness in deepening your capacity to dwell in stillness; to sit for longer periods of time; to sit in the face of adversity, difficulties, and storms or drabness in the mind. Ask yourself what you are learning from your experiments with this practice. Can you see some subtle transformation occurring in your attitude toward things that change in your life? Can you carry the mountain image with you in daily life? Can you see the mountain in others, and allow them their own shape and form, each mountain uniquely itself?

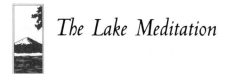

The Lake Meditation

The mountain image is only one of many that you may find supports your practice and makes it more vivid and elemental. Images of trees, rivers, clouds, sky can be useful allies as well. The image itself is not fundamental, but it can deepen and expand your view of practice.

Some people find the image of a lake particularly helpful. Because a lake is an expanse of water, the image lends itself to the lying-down posture, although it can be practiced sitting up as well. We know that the water principle is every bit as elemental as rock, and that its nature is stronger than rock in the sense that water wears down rock. Water also has the enchanting quality of receptivity. It parts to allow anything in, then resumes itself. If you hit a mountain or a rock with a hammer, in spite of its hardness, or actually because of it, the rock chips, fragments, breaks apart. But if you hit the ocean or a pond with a hammer, all you get is a rusty hammer. A key virtue of water power reveals itself in this.

To practice using the lake image in your meditation, picture in your mind's eye a lake, a body of water held in a receptive basin by the earth itself. Note in the mind's eye and in your own heart that water likes to pool in low places. It seeks its own level, asks to be contained. The lake you invoke may be deep or shallow, blue or green, muddy or clear. With no wind, the surface of the lake is flat. Mirrorlike, it reflects trees, rocks, sky, and clouds, holds everything in itself momentarily. Wind stirs up waves on the lake, from ripples to chop. Clear reflections disappear. But sunlight may still sparkle in the ripples and dance on the waves in a play of shimmering diamonds. When night comes, it's the moon's turn to dance on the lake, or if the surface is still, to be reflected in it along with the outline of trees and shadows. In winter, the lake may freeze over, yet teem with movement and life below.

When you have established a picture of the lake in your mind's eye, allow yourself to become one with the lake as you lie down on your back or sit in meditation, so that your energies are held by your awareness and by your openness and compassion for yourself in the same way as the lake's waters are held by the receptive and accepting basin of the earth herself. Breathing with the lake image moment by moment, feeling its body as your body, allow your mind and your heart to be open and receptive, to reflect whatever comes near. Experience the moments of complete stillness when both reflection and water are completely clear, and other moments when the surface is disturbed, choppy, stirred up, reflections and depth lost for a time. Through it all, as you dwell in meditation, simply noting the play of the various energies of your own mind and heart, the fleeting thoughts and feelings, impulses and reactions which come and go as ripples and waves, noting their effects just as you observe the various changing energies at play on the lake: the wind, the waves, the light and shadow and reflections, the colors, the smells.

Do your thoughts and feelings disturb the surface? Is that okay with you? Can you see a rippled or wavy surface as an intimate, essential aspect of being a lake, of having a surface? Can you identify not only with the surface but with the entire *body* of the water, so that you become the stillness below the surface as well, which at most experiences only gentle undulations, even when the surface is whipped to frothing?

In the same way, in your meditation practice and in your daily life, can you identify not only with the content of your thoughts and feelings but also with the vast unwavering reservoir of awareness itself residing below the surface of the mind? In the lake meditation, we sit with the intention to hold in awareness and acceptance all the qualities of mind and body, just as the lake sits held, cradled, contained by the earth, reflecting sun, moon, stars, trees, rocks, clouds, sky, birds, light, caressed by the air and wind, which bring out and highlight its sparkle, its vitality, its essence.

*

In such a day, in September or October, Walden is a perfect forest mirror, set round with stones as precious to my eye as if fewer or rarer. Nothing so fair, so pure, and at the same time so large, as a lake, perchance, lies on the surface of the earth. Sky water. It needs no fence. Nations come and go without defiling it. It is a mirror which no stone can crack, whose quicksilver will never wear off, whose gilding Nature continually repairs; no storms, no dust, can dim its surface ever fresh;—a mirror in which all impurity presented to it sinks, swept and dusted by the sun's hazy brush,—this the light dust-cloth,—which retains no breath that is breathed on it, but sends its own to float as clouds high above its surface, and be reflected in its bosom still.

THOREAU, *Walden*

TRY: Using the lake image to support sitting or lying in stillness, not going anywhere, held and cradled in awareness. Note when the mind reflects; when it is embroiled. Note the calm below the surface. Does this image suggest new ways of carrying yourself in times of turmoil?

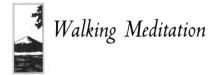

Walking Meditation

Peace is every step.

THICH NHAT HANH,
Peace Is Every Step

I know people who at one time found it very difficult to sit but got deeply into meditation practice through walking. No matter who you are, you can't sit all the time. And some people just find it virtually impossible to stay seated and mindful with the levels of pain and agitation and anger they feel. But they can walk with it.

In traditional monastic settings, periods of sitting meditation are interspersed with periods of walking meditation. They are the same practice. The walking is just as good as the sitting. What is important is how you keep your mind.

In formal walking meditation, you attend to the walking itself. You can focus on the footfall as a whole; or isolated segments of the motion such as shifting, moving, placing, shifting; or on the whole body moving. You can couple an awareness of walking with an awareness of breathing.

In walking meditation, you are not walking to get anyplace. Usually it is just back and forth in a lane, or round and round in a loop. Literally having no place to go makes it easier to be where you are. What's the point of trying to be somewhere else on your walking path when it really is all the same? The challenge is, can you be fully with *this* step, with *this* breath?

Walking meditation can be practiced at any pace, from ultra-slow to very brisk. How much of the foot cycle you can attend to will depend on the speed. The practice is to take each step as it comes and to be fully present with it. This means *feeling* the very sensations of walking—in your feet, in your legs, in your carriage and gait, as always, moment by moment, and in this case, step by step as well. You might call it "watching your step," pun intended, although it is an inner watching. You're not looking at your feet!

Just as in the sitting meditation, things will come up which will pull your attention away from the bare experience of walking. We work with those perceptions, thoughts, feelings and impulses, memories and anticipations, that come up during the walking in the very same way that we do in sitting meditation. Ultimately, walking is stillness in motion, flowing mindfulness.

It's best to do formal walking meditation in a place where you won't become a spectacle to other people, especially if you are going to do it very slowly. Good places are your living room, fields, or a clearing in the woods; isolated beaches are good, too. Push a shopping cart in front of you through a supermarket and you can walk as slowly as you like.

You can practice walking meditation informally anywhere. Informal walking meditation doesn't involve pacing back and forth or going around a loop, but just walking normally. You can walk mindfully along a sidewalk, down a corridor at work, going for a hike, walking your dog, walking with children. It involves recalling that you are here in your body. You simply remind yourself to be in this moment, taking each step as it comes, accepting each moment as it comes. If you find yourself rushing or becoming impatient, slowing the pace can help take the edge off your rushing and remind you that you are here now, and that when you get there, you will be there. If you miss the *here*, you are likely also to miss the *there*. If your mind is not centered here, it is likely not to be centered just because you arrive somewhere else.

TRY: Bringing awareness to walking, wherever you find yourself. Slow it down a bit. Center yourself in your body and in the present moment. Appreciate the fact that you are able to walk, which many people cannot. Perceive how miraculous it is, and for a moment, don't take for granted that your body works so wonderfully. Know that you are ambulating upright on the face of Mother Earth. Walk with dignity and confidence, and as the Navaho saying goes, walk in beauty, wherever you are.

Try walking formally as well. Before or after you sit, try a period of walking meditation. Keep a continuity of mindfulness between the walking and the sitting. Ten minutes is good, or half an hour. Remember once again that it is not clock time we are concerned with here. But you will learn more and understand walking meditation more deeply if you challenge yourself to keep at it past your first or second impulse to stop.

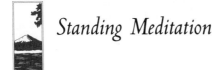

Standing Meditation

Standing meditation is best learned from trees. Stand close to one, or, better still, in a stand of trees and just peer out in one direction. Feel your feet developing roots into the ground. Feel your body sway gently, as it always will, just as trees do in a breeze. Staying put, in touch with your breathing, drink in what is in front of you, or keep your eyes closed and sense your surroundings. Sense the tree closest to you. Listen to it, feel its presence, touch it with your mind and body.

Use your breath to help you to stay in the moment . . . feeling your own body standing, breathing, being, moment by moment.

When mind or body first signals that perhaps it is time to move on, stay with the standing a while longer, remembering that trees stand still for years, occasionally lifetimes if they are fortunate. See if they do not have something to teach you about stillness and about being in touch. After all, they are touching the ground with roots and trunk, the air with trunk and branches, sunlight and the wind with their leaves; everything about a standing tree speaks of being in touch. Experiment with standing this way yourself, even for short periods of time. Work at being in touch with the air on your skin, the feel of the feet in contact with the ground, the sounds of the world, the dance of light and color and shadow, the dance of the mind.

TRY: Standing like this wherever you find yourself, in the woods, in the mountains, by a river, in your living room, or just waiting for the bus. When you are alone, you might try opening your palms to the sky and holding your arms out in various positions, like branches and leaves, accessible, open, receptive, patient.

Lying-Down Meditation

Lying down is a wonderful way to meditate if you can manage not to fall asleep. And if you do fall asleep, your sleep may be more restful if you enter it through meditation. You can wake up from sleeping in the same way, bringing full awareness to those first moments of wakefulness returning.

When your body is lying down, you can really let the whole of it go much more easily than you can in any other posture. Your body can sink into the bed, mat, floor, or ground until your muscles stop making the slightest effort to hold you together. This is a profound letting go at the level of your muscles and the motor neurons which govern them. The mind quickly follows if you give it permission to stay open and wakeful.

Using the body as a whole as the object of your attention in lying-down meditation is a blessing. You can feel the body from head to toe, breathing and radiating warmth over the entire envelope of your skin. It's the whole body that breathes, the whole body that is alive. In bringing mindfulness to the body as a whole, you can reclaim your entire body as the locus of your being and your vitality, and remind yourself that "you," whoever you are, are not just a resident of your head.

You can also focus on different areas in either a free-flowing or a more systematic way when practicing meditation lying down. We introduce the people in our clinic to lying-down meditation in the form of a forty-five-minute *body scan*. Not everybody can sit for forty-five minutes right away but anybody can do the body scan. All you need to do is lie here and feel different regions of your body and then let go of them. The body scan is systematic in the sense that we move through the various regions of the body in a particular order. But there is no one way to do it. It could be done scanning from head to feet or from feet to head or from side to side for that matter.

One way to practice is to inwardly direct your breath in to and out from the various regions of your body as if you could breathe right in to your toes or your knee, or your ear, and breathe out "from" those places. When you feel ready, on an outbreath you just let go of that region, allowing/inviting it to dissolve in your mind's eye (your imagination) as the muscles themselves let go and you drop into stillness and open awareness before moving on and connecting with the next region of the body, which you would come to on another inbreath. As much as possible, allow all the breathing to be through your nose.

You don't have to do lying-down meditation as systematically as in the body scan, however. You can also focus on particular regions of your body at will, or as they become dominant in the field of your awareness, perhaps due to pain or a problem with a particular region. Entering into them with openness and attention and acceptance can be profoundly healing, especially if you practice regularly. It feels like a deep nourishing of cells and tissues as well as of psyche and spirit, whole body and soul.

Lying-down meditation is a good way to get in touch with your emotional body, too. We possess a metaphorical, a mythical heart as well as a physical one. When we focus on the region of the heart, it can be helpful to tune in to any sensations of constriction in the chest, tightness, or heaviness, and be aware of emotions such as grief, sadness, loneliness, despair, unworthiness, or anger which may lie just beneath the surface of those physical sensations. We speak of broken hearts, of being hard-hearted or heavy-hearted, because the heart is known in our culture as the seat of our emotional life. The heart is also the seat of love, joy, and compassion, and such emotions are equally deserving of attention and of honoring as you discover them.

A number of specialized meditative practices such as loving kindness meditation are specifically oriented toward cultivating in oneself particular feeling states that expand and open the metaphorical heart. Acceptance, forgiveness, loving kindness, generosity, and trust all are strengthened by intentionally centering and sustaining attention in the heart region, and invoking such feelings as part of formal meditation practice. But these feelings are also strengthened through simply recognizing them when they arise spontaneously in your meditation practice and by encountering them with awareness.

Other body regions, too, have metaphorical meaning and can be approached in meditations, lying down and otherwise, with this kind of awareness. The solar plexus has a sunlike, radiant quality and can help us to contact feelings of centeredness, lying as it does at the center of gravity of the body, and of vitality (digestive fires). The throat vocalizes our emotions and can be either constricted or open. Feelings can get "stuck in the throat" sometimes, even if the heart is open. When we develop mindfulness of the throat region, it can put us more in touch with our speech and its tonal qualities—such as explosiveness, speed, harshness, volume, automaticity on the one hand, or softness, gentleness, sensitivity on the other—as well as its content.

Each region of the physical body has its counterpart in an emotional body or map which carries a deeper meaning for us, often completely below our level of awareness. In order to continue growing, we need to continuously activate, listen to, and learn from our emotional body. Lying-down meditations can help a lot with this as long as when you get up you are willing to risk the stands that your insights might require. In the old days, our cultures, mythologies, and rituals helped in the process of activating our emotional body and honoring its vitality and its impermanence. Usually this was done in same-sex initiation practices organized by the community of elders, whose job it was to educate the adolescents about what it meant to be a full adult within the tribe or culture. The importance of the development of the emotional body is hardly recognized today. We are pretty much left to our own devices to come to full adulthood, whether man or woman. Our elders may have become so denatured themselves from a lack of such nurturance that there is no longer a collective knowledge of how to guide the awakening emotional vitality and authenticity of our young people, our children. Mindfulness may contribute to a reawakening of this ancient wisdom in ourselves and in others.

Since we lie down for so much of our lives, lying-down meditation provides a readily accessible gateway to another dimension of consciousness. Before sleep, upon waking, while resting or lounging, the lying down can itself invite you to practice mindfulness, bringing breath and body together moment by moment, filling your body with awareness and acceptance, listening, listening, hearing, hearing, growing, growing, letting go, letting be . . .

TRY: Tuning in to your breath when you find yourself lying down. Feel it moving in your entire body. Dwell with the breath in various regions of your body, such as the feet, the legs, the pelvis and genitals, the belly, the chest, the back, the shoulders, the arms, the throat and neck, the head, the face, the top of your head. Listen carefully. Allow yourself to feel whatever is present. Watch the sensations in the body flux and change. Watch your feelings about them flux and change.

Try meditating on purpose lying down, not just around bedtime. Do it out of bed, on the floor, at different times of the day. Do it in fields and meadows on occasion, under trees, in the rain, in the snow.

Bring particular attention to your body as you are going to sleep and as you are waking up. Even for a few minutes, stretch yourself out straight, on your back if possible, and just feel the body as a whole breathing. Give special attention to any regions that are problematic for you and work at letting the breath invite them back into a sense of membership and wholeness with the rest of your body. Keep your emotional body in mind. Honor "gut" feelings.

Getting Your Body Down on the Floor at Least Once a Day

There is a particular feeling of time stopping when you get your body down on the floor, whether it's to practice a lying-down meditation such as the body scan or to systematically work the body gently but firmly toward its limits in first this direction, then that, as we do in mindful hatha yoga. Just being low down in a room tends to clear the mind. Maybe it's because being on the floor is so foreign to us that it breaks up our habitual neurological patterning and invites us to enter into this moment through a sudden opening in what we might call the body door.

In hatha yoga practice, the idea is to be fully in your body as you bring awareness to the various sensations, thoughts, and feelings which come up while you are moving, stretching, breathing, holding positions, reaching or lifting with arms, legs, and torso. There are said to be over 80,000 basic yoga postures. One won't quickly run out of new challenges for the body; but I find I keep coming back to a core routine of maybe twenty or so postures, which over the years just keep taking me deeper into my body and deeper into stillness.

Yoga folds movement and stillness into one another. It is a wonderfully nourishing practice. As in the other forms of mindfulness practice, you are not trying to get anywhere. But you *are* purposefully moving right up to the very limits of your body in this moment. You are exploring a terrain where there may be considerable intensity of sensation associated with stretching or lifting or maintaining your balance in unusual spatial configurations of limbs, head, and trunk. There you dwell, usually for longer than part of your mind would like, just breathing, just feeling your body. You are not looking to break through to anything. You are not competing with anybody else's body or even aiming to improve your own. You are not judging how your body is doing. You are simply residing in stillness, within the full range of your experiences, including any intensity or discomfort (which should in any case be benign if you have not forced yourself to go beyond your limits), tasting the bloom of these moments in your body.

All the same, for the devoted practitioner, it's hard not to notice that the body loves a steady diet of this and changes on its own. There is frequently an "on the way to" quality to this practice at the same time that there is the "just as it is now" feeling as the body sinks more and more deeply into a stretch or into letting go, lying on the floor between more effortful postures. Not forcing anything, we just do our best to line up with the warp and woof of body and mind, floor, and world, staying in touch.

T R Y : Getting down on the floor once a day and stretching your body mindfully, if only for three or four minutes, staying in touch with your breathing and with what your body is telling you. Remind yourself that this is your body today. Check to see if you are in touch with it.

Not Practicing Is Practicing

Sometimes I like to point out that not doing yoga is the same as doing yoga, although I hope people don't get the wrong idea and think I am saying it's the same whether you practice or not. What I mean is simply that every time you come back to yoga practice, you see the effect of not having done it for a while. So in a way you learn more by coming back to it than you would by just keeping it up.

Of course, this is only true if you notice things such as how still your body feels, how hard it is to hold a posture, how impatient the mind becomes, how it resists staying on the breath. These things are really hard *not* to notice when you are down on the floor holding on to your knee as you draw your head up toward it. They are much harder to be aware of when it's life itself that we are talking about rather than yoga. But the same principle applies. Yoga and life are different ways of saying the same thing. Forgetting or neglecting to be mindful can teach you a lot more than just being mindful all the time. Fortunately, most of us don't have to worry on that score, since our tendencies toward mindlessness are so robust. It is in the coming back to mindfulness that seeing lies.

T R Y : Noticing the difference in how you feel and how you handle stress in periods when you are into the discipline of daily meditation and yoga practice and in periods of your life when you are not. See if you can become aware of the consequences of your more mindless and automatic behaviors, especially when they are provoked by pressures stemming from work or home life. How do you carry yourself in your body in those periods when you are practicing and when you are not? What happens to your commitment to remember non-doing? How does the lack of regular practice affect your anxiety about time and about achieving certain results? How does it affect your relationships? Where do some of your most mindless patterns come from? What triggers them? Are you ready to hold them in awareness as they grip you by the throat, whether your formal practice is strong this week or not? Can you see that not practicing is an arduous practice?

Loving Kindness Meditation

No man is an Island, entire of it self;
Every man is a piece of the continent, a part of the main;
If a clod be washed away by the sea,
Europe is the less, as well as if a promontory were,
As well as if a manor of thy friends or of thine own were;
Any man's death diminishes me, because I am involved in
mankind;
And therefore, never send to know for whom the bell tolls;
It tolls for thee.

JOHN DONNE, *Meditation XVII*

We resonate with one another's sorrows because we are inter-connected. Being whole and simultaneously part of a larger whole, we can change the world simply by changing ourselves. If I become a center of love and kindness in this moment, then in a perhaps small but hardly insignificant way, the world now has a nucleus of love and kindness it lacked the moment before. This benefits me and it benefits others.

You may have noticed that you are not always a center of love and kindness, even toward yourself. In fact, in our society, one might speak of an epidemic of low self-esteem. In conversations with the Dalai Lama during a meeting in Dharamsala in 1990, he did a double take when a Western psychologist spoke of low self-esteem. The phrase had to be translated several times for him into Tibetan, although his English is quite good. He just couldn't grasp the notion of low self-esteem, and when he finally understood what was being said, he was visibly saddened to hear that so many people in America carry deep feelings of self-loathing and inadequacy.

Such feelings are virtually unheard of among the Tibetans. They have all the severe problems of refugees from oppression living in the Third World, but low self-esteem is not one of them. But who knows what will happen to future generations as they come into contact with what we ironically call the "developed world." Maybe we are overdeveloped outwardly and underdeveloped inwardly. Perhaps it is we who, for all our wealth, are living in poverty.

You can take steps to rectify this poverty through loving kindness meditation. As usual, the place to begin is with yourself. Might you invite a sense of kindness and acceptance and cherishing to arise in your own heart? You would have to do so over and over again, you know, just as you would bring your mind back to the breath over and over again in the sitting meditation. The mind won't take easily to it, because the wounds we carry run deep. But you might try, just as an experiment, to hold yourself in awareness and acceptance for a time in your practice, as a mother would hold a hurt or frightened child, with a completely available and unconditional love. Can you cultivate forgiveness of yourself, if not of others? Is it even possible to invite yourself to be happy in this moment? Is it okay for you to feel okay? Is the basis of happiness present in this moment at all?

Loving kindness practice is done in the following way, but please don't mistake the words for the practice. As usual, they are just signposts pointing the way:

Start by centering yourself in your posture and in your breathing. Then, from your heart or from your belly, invite feelings or images of kindness and love to radiate until they fill your whole being. Allow yourself to be cradled by your own awareness as if you were as deserving of loving kindness as any child. Let your awareness embody both benevolent mother energy and benevolent father energy, making available for you in this moment a recognition and an honoring of your being, and a kindness you perhaps did not receive enough of as a child. Let yourself bask in this energy of loving kindness, breathing it in and breathing it out, as if it were a lifeline, long in disrepair but finally passing along a nourishment you were starving for.

Invite feelings of peacefulness and acceptance to be present in you. Some people find it valuable to say to themselves from time to time such things as: "May I be free from ignorance. May I be free from greed and hatred. May I not suffer. May I be happy." But the words are just meant to evoke feelings of loving kindness. They are a wishing oneself well—consciously formed intentions to be free now, in this moment at least, from the problems we so often make for ourselves or compound for ourselves through our own fear and forgetfulness.

Once you have established yourself as a center of love and kindness radiating throughout your being, which amounts to a cradling of yourself in loving kindness and acceptance, you can dwell here indefinitely, drinking at this fount, bathing in it, renewing yourself, nourishing yourself, enlivening yourself. This can be a profoundly healing practice for body and soul.

You can also take the practice further. Having established a radiant center in your being, you can let loving kindness radiate outwardly and direct it wherever you like. You might first direct it toward the members of your immediate family. If you have children, hold them in your mind's eye and in your heart, visualizing their essential selves, wishing them well, that they not suffer needlessly, that they come to know their true way in the world, that they may experience love and acceptance in life. And then including, as you go along, a partner, spouse, siblings, parents. . . .

You can direct loving kindness toward your parents whether they are alive or dead, wishing them well, wishing that they may not feel isolated or in pain, honoring them. If you feel capable of it and it feels healthy to you, and liberating, finding a place in your own heart to forgive them for their limitations, for their fears, and for any wrong actions and suffering they may have caused, remembering Yeats's line, "Why, what could she have done, being what she is?"

And there's no need to stop here. You can direct loving kindness toward anybody, toward people you know and people you don't. It may benefit them, but it will certainly benefit you by refining and extending your emotional being. This extension matures as you purposefully direct loving kindness toward people you have a hard time with, toward those you dislike or are repulsed by, toward those who threaten you or have hurt you. You can also practice directing loving kindness toward whole groups of people—toward all those who are oppressed, or who suffer, or whose lives are caught up in war or violence or hatred, understanding that they are not different from you—that they too have loved ones, hopes and aspirations, and needs for shelter, food, and peace. And you can extend loving kindness to the planet itself, its glories and its silent suffering, to the environment, the streams and rivers, to the air, the oceans, the forests, to plants and animals, collectively or singly.

There is really no natural limit to the practice of loving kindness in meditation or in one's life. It is an ongoing, ever-expanding realization of interconnectedness. It is also its embodiment. When you can love one tree or one flower or one dog or one place, or one person or yourself for one moment, you can find all people, all places, all suffering, all harmony in that one moment. Practicing in this way is not trying to change anything or get anywhere, although it might look like it on the surface. What it is really doing is uncovering what is always present. Love and kindness are here all the time, somewhere, in fact, everywhere. Usually our ability to touch them and be touched by them lies buried below our own fears and hurts, below our greed and our hatreds, below our desperate clinging to the illusion that we are truly separate and alone.

By invoking such feelings in our practice, we are stretching against the edges of our own ignorance, just as in the yoga we stretch against the resistance of muscle, ligament, and tendon, and as in that and all other forms of meditation, against the boundaries and ignorance of our own minds and hearts. And in the stretching, painful as it sometimes is, we expand, we grow, we change ourselves, we change the world.

*

My religion is kindness.

THE DALAI LAMA

T R Y: Touching base with feelings of loving kindness within yourself at some point in your meditation practice. See if you can get behind any objections you may have to this practice, or behind your reasons for being unlovable or unacceptable. Just look at all that as thinking. Experiment with allowing yourself to bathe in the warmth and acceptance of loving kindness as if you were a child held in a loving mother's or father's arms. Then play with directing it toward others and out into the world. There is no limit to this practice, but as with any other practice, it deepens and grows with constant attending, like plants in a lovingly tended garden. Make sure that you are not *trying* to help anybody else or the planet. Rather, you are simply holding them in awareness, honoring them, wishing them well, opening to their pain with kindness and compassion and acceptance. If, in the process, you find that this practice calls you to act differently in the world, then let those actions too embody loving kindness and mindfulness.

Part Three

In the Spirit of Mindfulness

All of us are apprenticed to the same teacher that the
religious institutions originally worked with: reality.
Reality-insight says . . . master the twenty-four hours.
Do it well, without self-pity. It is as hard to get the children
herded into the car pool and down the road to the bus as
it is to chant sutras in the Buddha-hall on a cold morning.
One move is not better than the other, each can be quite
boring, and they both have the virtuous quality of repetition.
Repetition and ritual and their good results come in
many forms. Changing the filter, wiping noses, going to
meetings, picking up around the house, washing dishes,
checking the dipstick—don't let yourself think these are
distracting you from your more serious pursuits.
Such a round of chores is not a set of difficulties we
hope to escape from so that we may do our "practice"
which will put us on a "path"—it *is* our path.

GARY SNYDER, *The Practice of the Wild*

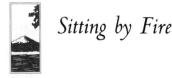

Sitting by Fire

In the old days, once the sun went down, the only source of light people had, other than the changing moon and firmament of stars, was fire. For millions of years, we human beings sat around fires, gazing into the flames and embers with cold and darkness at our backs. Maybe this is where formal meditation first got its start.

Fire was a comfort to us, our source of heat, light, and protection—dangerous but, with great care, controllable. Sitting by it gave us relaxation at the end of the day. In its warm, flickering light, we could tell stories and talk about the day past, or just sit silently, seeing the reflection of our minds in the ever-changing flames and the glowing landscapes of a magical world. Fire made the darkness bearable, and helped us feel secure and safe. It was calming, reliable, restoring, meditative, and absolutely necessary for survival.

This necessity has flown from our everyday lives, and with it almost all occasion to be still. In today's fast-paced world, fires are impractical or an occasional luxury to set a certain mood. We have only to flip a switch when the outer light begins to dim. We can light up the world as brightly as we want and keep going with our lives, filling all our waking hours with busyness, with doing. Life gives us scant time for being nowadays, unless we seize it on purpose. We no longer have a fixed time when we have to stop what we are doing because there's not enough light to do it by . . . we lack that formerly built-in time we had every night for shifting gears, for letting go of the day's activities. We have precious few occasions nowadays for the mind to settle itself in stillness by a fire.

Instead, we watch television at the end of the day, a pale electronic fire energy, and pale in comparison. We submit ourselves to constant bombardment by sounds and images that come from minds other than our own, that fill our heads with information and trivia, other people's adventures and excitement and desires. Watching television leaves even less room in the day for experiencing stillness. It soaks up time, space, and silence, a soporific, lulling us into mindless passivity. "Bubble gum for the eyes," Steve Allen called it. Newspapers do much the same. They are not bad in themselves, but we frequently conspire to use them to rob ourselves of many precious moments in which we might be living more fully.

It turns out that we don't have to succumb to the addictive appeals of external absorptions in entertainment and passionate distraction. We can develop other habits that bring us back to that elemental yearning inside ourselves for warmth, stillness, and inner peace. When we sit with our breathing, for instance, it is much like sitting by fire. Looking deeply into the breath, we can see at least as much as in glowing coals and embers and flames, reflections of our own mind dancing. A certain warmth is generated, too. And if we are truly not trying to get anywhere but simply allow ourselves to be here in this moment as it is, we can stumble easily upon an ancient stillness—behind and within the play of our thoughts and feelings—that in a simpler time, people found in sitting by the fire.

Harmony

As I pull into the parking lot of the hospital, several hundred geese pass overhead. They are flying high and I do not hear their honking. What strikes me first is that they clearly know where they are going. They are flying northwest, and there are so many of them that the formation trails out far to the east, where the early November sun is hugging the horizon. As the first of them fly over, I am moved by the nobility and beauty of their purposeful assembly to grab paper and pen right there in the car and capture the pattern as best my unskilled hand and eye are able. Rapid strokes suffice . . . they will shortly be gone.

Hundreds are in V's, but many are in more complex arrangements. Everything is in motion. Their lines dip and ascend with grace and harmony, like a cloth waving in the air. It is clear that they are communicating. Each one somehow knows where it is, has a place in this complex and constantly changing pattern, belongs.

I feel strangely blessed by their passage. This moment is a gift. I have been permitted to see and share in something I know is important, something I am not graced with that often. Part of it is their wildness, part is the harmony, order, and beauty they embody.

My usual experience of time flowing is suspended while

witnessing their passing. The pattern is what scientists call "chaotic," like cloud formations or the shapes of trees. There is order, and within it, embedded disorder, yet that too is orderly. For me now, it is simply the gift of wonder and amazement. Nature is showing me as I come to work today how things actually are in one small sphere, reminding me how little we humans know, and how little we appreciate harmony, or even see it.

And so, reading the newspaper that evening, I note that the full consequences of logging the rain forests covering the high ground in the South Philippines were not apparent until the typhoon of late 1991 struck, when the denuded earth, no longer able to hold water, let it rush unchecked to the lowlands at four times the usual volume and drowned thousands of poor inhabitants of the region. As the popular bumper sticker says, "Shit happens." The trouble is, too often we are unwilling see our role in it. There are definite risks to disdaining the harmony of things.

Nature's harmony is around us and within us at all times. Perceiving it is an occasion for great happiness; but it is often only appreciated in retrospect or in its absence. If all is going well in the body, it tends to go unnoticed. Your lack of a headache is not front-page news for your cerebral cortex. Abilities such as walking, seeing, thinking, and peeing take care of themselves, and so blend into the landscape of automaticity and unawareness. Only pain or fear or loss wake us and bring things into focus. But by then the harmony is harder to see, and we find ourselves caught up in turbulence, itself containing, like rapids and waterfalls, order of a more difficult and subtle level within the river of life. As Joni Mitchell sings, "You don't know what you've got till it's gone . . ."

As I get out of the car, I inwardly bow to these wayfarers for anointing the airspace of this necessarily civilized hospital parking lot with a refreshing dose of natural wildness.

T R Y: Drawing back the veil of unawareness to perceive harmony in this moment. Can you see it in clouds, in sky, in people, in the weather, in food, in your body, in this breath? Look, and look again, right here, right now!

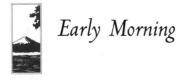

Early Morning

Even though he had no job to go to, no children to feed and get off to school, no external reasons to get up early, it was Thoreau's custom, for the time he lived at Walden, to wake early in the morning and bathe in the pond at dawn. He did it for inner reasons, as a spiritual discipline in itself: "It was a religious exercise, and one of the best things I did."

Benjamin Franklin also extolled the virtues of health, wealth, and wisdom obtained from waking up early in his well-known adage on the subject. But he didn't mouth it; he practiced too.

The virtues of getting up early have nothing to do with cramming more hours of busyness and industry into one's day. Just the opposite. They stem from the stillness and solitude of the hour, and the potential to use that time to expand consciousness, to contemplate, to make time for being, for purposefully *not* doing anything. The peacefulness, the darkness, the dawn, the stillness—all contribute to making early morning a special time for mindfulness practice.

Waking early has the added value of giving you a very real head start on the day. If you can begin your day with a firm foundation in mindfulness and inner peacefulness, then when you do have to get going and start doing, it is much more likely that the doing will flow out of your being. You are more likely to carry a robust mindfulness, an inner calmness and balance of mind with you throughout the day, than had you just jumped out of bed and started in on the call of demands and responsibilities, however pressing and important.

The power of waking up early in the morning is so great that it can have a profound effect on a person's life, even without formal mindfulness practice. Just witnessing the dawn each day is a wake-up call in itself.

But I find early morning a wondrous time for formal meditation. No one else is up. The world's rush hasn't launched itself yet. I get out of bed and usually devote about an hour to being, without doing anything. After twenty-eight years, it hasn't lost its allure. On occasion it is difficult to wake up and either my mind or my body resists. But part of the value is in doing it anyway, even if I don't feel like it.

One of the principal virtues of a daily discipline is an acquired transparency toward the appeals of transitory mood states. A commitment to getting up early to meditate becomes independent of wanting or not wanting to do so on any particular morning. The practice calls us to a higher standard—that of remembering the importance of wakefulness and the ease with which we can slip into a pattern of automatic living which lacks awareness and sensitivity. Just waking up early to practice nondoing is itself a tempering process. It generates enough heat to rearrange our atoms, gives us a new and stronger crystal lattice of mind and body, a lattice that keeps us honest and reminds us that there is far more to life than getting things done.

Discipline provides a constancy which is independent of what kind of a day you had yesterday and what kind of a day you anticipate today. I especially try to make time for formal practice, if just for a few minutes, on days when momentous events happen, happy or distressing, when my mind and the circumstances are in turmoil, when there is lots to be done and feelings are running strong. In this way, I am less likely to miss the inner meaning of such moments, and I might even navigate through them a bit better.

By grounding yourself in mindfulness early in the morning, you are reminding yourself that things are always changing, that good and bad things come and go, and that it is possible to embody a perspective of constancy, wisdom, and inner peace as you face *any* conditions that present themselves. Making the daily choice to wake up early to practice is an embodiment of this perspective. I sometimes speak of it as my "routine," but it is far from routine. Mindfulness is the very opposite of routine.

If you are reluctant to get up an hour earlier than you ordinarily might, you can always try half an hour, or fifteen minutes, or even five minutes. It's the spirit that counts. Even five minutes of mindfulness practice in the morning can be valuable. And even five minutes of sacrificed sleep is likely to put you in touch with just how attached we are to sleep, and therefore how much discipline and resolve are required to carve out even that little time for ourselves to be awake without doing anything. After all, the thinking mind always has the very credible-sounding excuse that since you will not be accomplishing anything and there's no real pressure to do it *this* morning, and perhaps real reasons not to, why not catch the extra sleep which you know you need now, and start tomorrow?

To overcome such totally predictable opposition from other corners of the mind, you need to decide the night before that you are going to wake up, no matter what your thinking comes up with. This is the flavor of true intentionality and inner discipline. You do it simply because you committed to yourself to do it, and you do it at the appointed time, whether part of the mind feels like it or not. After a while, the discipline becomes a part of you. It's simply the new way you choose to live. It is not a "should," it doesn't involve forcing yourself. Your values and your actions have simply shifted.

If you are not ready for that yet (or even if you are), you can always use the very moment of waking up, no matter what time it comes, as a moment of mindfulness, the very first of the new day. Before you even move, try getting in touch with the fact that your breath is moving. Feel your body lying in bed. Straighten it out. Ask yourself, "Am I awake now? Do I know that the gift of a new day is being given to me? Will I be awake for it? What will happen today? Right now I don't really know. Even as I think about what I have to do, can I be open to this not-knowing? Can I see today as an adventure? Can I see right now as filled with possibilities?"

✳

Morning is when I am awake and there is a dawn in me. . . . We must learn to reawaken and keep ourselves awake, not by mechanical aids, but by an infinite expectation of the dawn, which does not forsake us in our soundest sleep. I know of no more encouraging fact than the unquestionable ability of man to elevate his life by conscious endeavor. It is something to be able to paint a particular picture, or to carve a statue, and so to make a few objects beautiful; but it is far more glorious to carve and paint the very atmosphere and medium though which we look. . . . To affect the quality of the day, that is the highest of arts.

THOREAU, *Walden*

TRY: Making a commitment to yourself to get up earlier than you otherwise might. Just doing it changes your life. Let that time, whatever its length, be a time of being, a time for intentional wakefulness. You don't want to fill this time with anything other than awareness. No need to go over the day's commitments in your head and live "ahead" of yourself. This is a time of no-time, of stillness, of presence, of being with yourself.

Also, at the moment of waking up, before getting out of bed, get in touch with your breath, feel the various sensations in your body, note any thoughts and feelings that may be present, let mindfulness touch this moment. Can you feel your breathing? Can you perceive the dawning of each in breath? Can you enjoy the feeling of the breath freely entering your body in this moment? Ask yourself: "Am I awake now?"

Direct Contact

We all carry around ideas and images of reality, frequently garnered from other people or from courses we have taken, books we have read, or from television, the radio, newspapers, the culture in general, which give us pictures of how things are and what is occurring. As a result, we often see our thoughts, or someone else's, instead of seeing what is right in front of us or inside of us. Often, we don't even bother to look or check how we feel because we think we already know and under-stand. So we can be closed to the wonder and vitality of fresh encounters. If we are not careful, we can even forget that di-rect contact is possible. We may lose touch with what is basic and not even know it. We can live in a dream reality of our own making without even a sense of the loss, the gulf, the unnecessary distance we place between ourselves and experi-ence. Not knowing this, we can be all the more impoverished, spiritually and emotionally. But something wonderful and unique can occur when our contact with the world becomes direct.

Viki Weisskopf, a mentor of mine and friend, and a re-nowned physicist, tells the following poignant story about direct contact:

Several years ago I received an invitation to give a series of lectures at the University of Arizona at Tucson. I was delighted to accept because it would give me a chance to visit the Kitts Peak astronomical observatory, which had a very powerful telescope I had always wanted to look through. I asked my hosts to arrange an evening to visit the observatory so I could look directly at some interesting objects through the telescope. But I was told this would be impossible because the telescope was constantly in use for photography and other research activities. There was no time for simply looking at objects. In that case, I replied, I would not be able to come to deliver my talks. Within days I was informed that everything had been arranged according to my wishes. We drove up the mountain on a wonderfully clear night. The stars and the Milky Way glistened intensely and seemed almost close enough to touch. I entered the cupola and told the technicians who ran the computer-activated telescope that I wanted to see Saturn and a number of the galaxies. It was a great pleasure to observe with my own eyes and with the utmost clarity all the details I had only seen on photographs before. As I looked at all that, I realized that the room had begun to fill with people, and one by one they too peeked into the telescope. I was told that these were astronomers attached to the observatory,

but they had never before had the opportunity of
looking directly at the objects of their investigations.
I can only hope that this encounter made them realize
the importance of such direct contacts.

VICTOR WEISSKOPF, *The Joy of Insight*

TRY: Thinking that your life is at least as interesting and
miraculous as the moon or the stars. What is it that stands
between you and direct contact with your life? What can you do
to change that?

Is There Anything Else You Would Like to Tell Me?

Of course, direct contact is hardly of minimal consequence in the doctor-patient relationship. We go to great lengths to help medical students understand the topology of this landscape, and not run away from it in terror because it involves their own feelings as individuals and the need to really listen empathically, treating patients as people rather than solely as disease puzzles and opportunities to exercise judgment and control. So many things can get in the way of direct contact. Many doctors lack formal training in this dimension of medicine. They remain unaware of the crucial importance of effective communication and caring in what we call health care but which too often is just disease care; and even good disease care can be sorely lacking if the subject is excluded from the equation.

My mother, exasperated at her inability to find a doctor willing to treat her concerns seriously, described how, at a follow-up visit initiated by her because she was still not walking well and was in a lot of pain, the orthopedic surgeon, who had replaced her hip with an artificial one, studied the X-ray, commenting how good it looked ("superb" was the word he used), and didn't make any attempt to examine her real, in-the-flesh hip and leg or to even acknowledge her complaint until she had insisted on it several times. And then, it held little weight—the

X-ray was enough to convince him that she shouldn't be having any pain—except she was.

Doctors can unknowingly hide behind their handiwork, their instruments, medical tests, and technical vocabulary. They may be reluctant to come into too direct contact with the patient as a whole person, an individual with unique thoughts and fears, values, cares, and questions, spoken and unspoken. They often doubt their own capacity to do this because it is such uncharted and potentially frightening territory. In part it may be that they are unaccustomed to looking at their own thoughts and fears, values, cares, and doubts so someone else's can feel pretty intimidating. And it may be that they don't feel they have time to open these potential floodgates, or that they doubt they would know how to respond adequately. But what is required most by patients is simply listening, being present, taking the *person* seriously, not just the disease.

To this end, we teach our medical students, among other things, to ask the open-ended question, "Is there anything else you would like to tell me?" at the end of the medical interview. We encourage them to pause, for quite a while if necessary, leaving the patient enough psychic space to consider his or her needs and perhaps the real agenda for being there. This is often not what gets talked about first or second, or even at all if the doctor isn't particularly tuned in or is in a hurry.

At a faculty development session one day, some experts from another institution were describing their training program for the medical interview, which uses videotaping to give the students direct feedback on their patient-interviewing style. At one point, they showed us a series of very short clips of just that last question being asked from a number of different interviews, each student simply asking one patient, "Is there anything else you would like to tell me?" Before showing these clips, we were assigned the task of noticing and later reporting on what was going on.

By the third one, I was doing everything I could to keep myself from rolling on the floor with laughter. To my surprise, there were a good many blank faces although some caught on quickly. The same thing was happening in clip after clip, but it was so obvious that it was hard to see, just like lots of things that are right under our noses.

In virtually every clip, while the student was saying what he or she had been taught to say to close the interview, namely: "Is there anything else you would like to tell me?", every single one was noticeably shaking his or her head from side to side, non-verbally conveying the message: "No, please, don't tell me any more!"

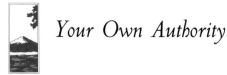

Your Own Authority

When I started work at the medical center, I was given three long white coats which have *"Dr. Kabat-Zinn / Department of Medicine"* neatly embroidered on the pocket. They have hung on the back of my door now for fifteen years, unused.

To me, these white coats are a symbol of exactly what I don't need in my job. I suppose they are a good thing for physicians, enhancing as they do the aura of authority and thus the positive placebo effect with their patients. The aura is augmented further if there is a stethoscope hanging out of the pocket at just the right angle. Young doctors sometimes try in their enthusiasm to go this one better and wear it with studied casualness across the back of the neck and shoulders.

But working in the stress reduction clinic, the white coat would be a true impediment. I have to work overtime as it is to reflect back all the projections I get from people that I am "Mr. Relaxation" or "Dr. Have-it-all-together" or "Mr. Wisdom and Compassion-incarnate." The whole point of mindfulness-based stress reduction—and for that matter health promotion in its largest sense—is to challenge and encourage people to become their own authorities, to take more responsibility for their own lives, their own bodies, their own health. I like to emphasize that each person is already the world authority on him- or herself, or at least could be if they started attending to things mindfully. A great deal of the information each of us needs to learn more about ourselves and our health—information we desperately need in order to grow and to heal and to make effective life choices—is already right at our fingertips, at the tips of, or rather, right beneath, our noses.

What is required to participate more fully in our own health and well-being is simply to listen more carefully and to trust what we hear, to trust the messages from our own life, from our own body and mind and feelings. This sense of participation and trust is all too frequently a missing ingredient in medicine. We call it "mobilizing the inner resources of the patient" for healing, or for just coping better, for seeing a little more clearly, for being a little more assertive, for asking more questions, for getting by more skillfully. It's not a replacement for expert medical care, but it is a necessary complement to it if you hope to live a truly healthy life—especially in the face of disease, disability, health challenges, and a frequently alienating, intimidating, insensitive, and sometimes iatrogenic health-care system.

Developing such an attitude means authoring one's own life and, therefore, assuming some measure of authority oneself. It requires believing in oneself. Deep down, sadly, a lot of us don't.

Mindful inquiry can heal low self-esteem, for the simple reason that a low self-estimation is really a wrong calculation, a misperception of reality. You can see this very clearly when you start to observe your own body or even just your breathing in meditation. You quickly come to see that even your body is miraculous. It performs amazing feats by the moment with no conscious effort. Our esteem problems stem in large part from our thinking, colored by past experiences. We see only our shortcomings and blow them out of all proportion. At the same time, we take all our good qualities for granted, or fail to acknowledge them at all. Perhaps we get stuck in the often deep and still bleeding wounds of childhood, and forget or never discover that we have golden qualities too. The wounds are important, but so are our inner goodness, our caring, our kindness toward others, the wisdom of the body, our capacity to think, to know what's what. And we do know what's what, much more than we allow. Yet, instead of seeing in a balanced way, we frequently persist in the habit of projecting onto others that *they* are okay and *we* are not.

I balk when people project onto me in this way. I try to reflect it back to them as commonsensically as I can, in the hope that they will come to see what they are doing and understand that their positive energy *for me* is really *theirs.* The positivity is their own. It is their energy, and they need to keep it and use it and appreciate its source. Why should they give away their power? I have enough problems of my own.

*

[People] measure their esteem of each other by what each has, and not by what each is. . . . Nothing can bring you peace but yourself.

RALPH WALDO EMERSON, *Self-Reliance*

Wherever You Go, There You Are

Have you ever noticed that there is no running away from anything? That, sooner or later, the things that you don't want to deal with and try to escape from, or paper over and pretend aren't there, catch up with you—especially if they have to do with old patterns and fears? The romantic notion is that if it's no good over here, you have only to go over there and things will be different. If this job is no good, change jobs. If this wife is no good, change wives. If this town is no good, change towns. If these children are a problem, leave them for other people to look after. The underlying thinking is that the reason for your troubles is outside of you—in the location, in others, in the circumstances. Change the location, change the circumstances, and everything will fall into place; you can start over, have a new beginning.

The trouble with this way of seeing is that it conveniently ignores the fact that you carry your head and your heart, and what some would call your "karma," around with you. You cannot escape yourself, try as you might. And what reason, other than pure wishful thinking, would you have to suspect that things would be different or better somewhere else anyway? Sooner or later, the same problems would arise if in fact they stem in large part from your patterns of seeing, thinking, and behaving. Too often, our lives cease working because we cease working at life, because we are unwilling to take responsibility for things as they are, and to work with our difficulties. We don't understand that it is actually possible to attain clarity, understanding, and transformation right in the middle of what is here and now, however problematic it may be. But it is easier and less threatening to our sense of self to project our involvement in our problems onto other people and the environment.

It is so much easier to find fault, to blame, to believe that what is needed is a change on the outside, an escape from the forces that are holding you back, preventing you from growing, from finding happiness. You can even blame yourself for it all and, in the ultimate escape from responsibility, run away feeling that you have made a hopeless mess of things, or that you are damaged beyond repair. In either case, you believe that you are incapable of true change or growth, and that you need to spare others any more pain by removing yourself from the scene.

The casualties of this way of looking at things are all over the place. Look virtually anywhere and you will find broken relationships, broken families, broken people—wanderers with no roots, lost, going from this place to that, this job to that, this relationship to that, this idea of salvation to that, in the desperate hope that the right person, the right job, the right place, the right book will make it all better. Or feeling isolated, unlovable, and in despair, having given up looking and even making any attempt, however misguided, to find peace of mind.

By itself, meditation does not confer immunity from this pattern of looking elsewhere for answers and solutions to one's problems. Sometimes people chronically go from one technique to another, or from teacher to teacher, or tradition to tradition, looking for that special something, that special teaching, that special relationship, that momentary "high" which will open the door to self-understanding and liberation. But this can turn into serious delusion, an unending quest to escape looking at what is closest to home and perhaps most painful. Out of fear and yearning for someone special to help them to see clearly, people sometimes fall into unhealthy dependency relationships with meditation teachers, forgetting that no matter how good the teacher, ultimately you have to live the inner work yourself, and that work always comes from the cloth of your own life.

Some people even wind up misusing teacher-led meditation retreats as a way to keep afloat in their lives rather than as an extended opportunity to look deeply into themselves. On retreat, in a certain way everything is easy. The bare necessities of living are taken care of. The world makes sense. All I have to do is sit and walk, be mindful, stay in the present, be cooked for and fed by a caring staff, listen to the great wisdom that is being put out by people who have worked deeply on themselves and have attained considerable understanding and harmony in their lives, and I will be transformed, inspired to live more fully myself, know how to be in the world, have a better perspective on my own problems.

To a large extent, this is all true. Good teachers and long periods of isolated meditation on retreat can be profoundly valuable and healing, *if* one is willing to look at everything that comes up during a retreat. But there is also the danger, which needs to be looked out for, that retreats can become a retreat from life in the world, and that one's "transformation" will, in the end, be only skin deep. Perhaps it will last a few days, weeks, or months after the retreat ends, then it's back to the same old pattern and lack of clarity in relationships, and looking forward to the next retreat, or the next great teacher, or a pilgrimage to Asia, or some other romantic fantasy in which things will deepen or become clearer and you will be a better person.

This way of thinking and seeing is an all-too-prevalent trap. There is no successful escaping from yourself in the long run, only transformation. It doesn't matter whether you are using drugs or meditation, alcohol or Club Med, divorce or quitting your job. There can be no resolution leading to growth until the present situation has been faced completely and you have opened to it with mindfulness, allowing the roughness of the situation itself to sand down your own rough edges. In other words, you must be willing to let life itself become your teacher.

This is the path of working where you find yourself, with what is found here and now. This, then, really is it . . . this place, this relationship, this dilemma, this job. The challenge of mindfulness is to work with the very circumstances that you find yourself in—no matter how unpleasant, how discouraging, how limited, how unending and stuck they may appear to be—and to make sure that you have done everything in your power to use their energies to transform yourself before you decide to cut your losses and move on. It is right here that the real work needs to happen.

So, if you think your meditation practice is dull, or no good, or that the conditions aren't right where you find yourself, and you think that if only you were in a cave in the Himalayas, or at an Asian monastery, or on a beach in the tropics, or at a retreat in some natural setting, things would be better, your meditation stronger . . . think again. When you got to your cave or your beach or your retreat, there you would be, with the same mind, the same body, the very same breath that you already have here. After fifteen minutes or so in the cave, you might get lonely, or want more light, or the roof might drip water on you. If you were on the beach, it might be raining or cold. If you were on retreat, you might not like the teachers, or the food, or your room. There is always something to dislike. So why not let go and admit that you might as well be at home wherever you are? Right in that moment, you touch the core of your being and invite mindfulness to enter and heal. If you understand this, then and only then will the cave, the monastery, the beach, the retreat center, offer up their true richness to you. But so will all other moments and places.

*

My foot slips on a narrow ledge: in that split second, as needles of fear pierce heart and temples, eternity intersects with present time. Thought and action are not different, and stone, air, ice, sun, fear, and self are one. What is exhilarating is to extend this acute awareness into ordinary moments, in the moment-by-moment experiencing of the lammergeier and the wolf, which, finding themselves at the center of things, have no need for any secret of true being. In this very breath that we take now lies the secret that all great teachers try to tell us, what one lama refers to as "the precision and openness and intelligence of the present." The purpose of meditation practice is not enlightenment; it is to pay attention even at un-extraordinary times, to be of the present, nothing-but-the-present, to bear this mindfulness of *now* into each event of ordinary life.

PETER MATTHIESSEN, *The Snow Leopard*

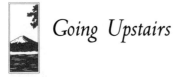

Going Upstairs

Occasions to practice mindfulness in daily life abound. Going upstairs is a good one for me. I do it hundreds of times a day when I'm at home. Usually I need something from upstairs, or to speak with someone upstairs, but my long-term agenda is to be downstairs, so I'm frequently torn between two places. I'm on my way up only to be on my way down, after I've found what I'm looking for, or gone to the bathroom, or whatever.

So I discover that I am frequently pulled by my need to be somewhere else, or by the next thing I think needs to happen, or the next place I think I'm supposed to be. When I find myself racing upstairs, usually two steps at a time, I sometimes have the presence of mind to catch myself in mid-frenetic dash. I become conscious of being slightly out of breath, aware that my heart is racing as well as my mind, that the whole of my being in that moment is being driven by some hurried purpose which often even eludes me by the time I'm up there.

When I am able to capture this wave of energy in aware-ness while I am still at the bottom of the stairs or starting on my way up, I will sometimes slow my ascent—not just one step at a time, but really slow, maybe one breath cycle per step, reminding myself that there is really no place I have to go and nothing I have to get that can't wait another moment for the sake of being fully in this one.

I find that when I remember to do this, I am more in touch along the way and more centered at the top. I also find that there is hardly ever an outward hurry. Only an inner one, usually driven by impatience and a mindless type of anxious thinking, which varies from so subtle I have to listen carefully to detect it at all, to so dominant that almost nothing will deflect its momentum. But even then, I can be aware of it and of its consequences, and this awareness by itself helps keep me from losing myself completely in the turbulence of the mind in those moments. And, as you might guess, this works going down the stairs too, but here, because the momentum of gravity is working for me, it's even more of a challenge to slow things down.

TRY: To use ordinary, repetitive occasions in your own house as invitations to practice mindfulness. Going to the front door, answering the telephone, seeking out someone else in the house to speak with, going to the bathroom, getting the laundry out of the dryer, going to the refrigerator, can all be occasions to slow down and be more in touch with each present moment. Notice the inner feelings which push you toward the telephone or the doorbell on the first ring. Why does your response time have to be so fast that it pulls you out of the life you were living in the preceding moment? Can these transitions become more graceful? Can you be more where you find yourself, all the time?

Also, try being present for things like taking a shower, or eating. When you are in the shower, are you really in the shower? Do you feel the water on your skin, or are you someplace else, lost in thought, missing the shower altogether? Eating is another good occasion for mindfulness practice. Are you tasting your food? Are you aware of how fast, how much, when, where, and what you are eating? Can you make your entire day as it unfolds into an occasion to be present or to bring yourself back to the present, over and over again?

Cleaning the Stove While Listening to Bobby McFerrin

I can lose myself and find myself simultaneously while cleaning the kitchen stove. This is a great, if rare occasion for mindfulness practice. Because I don't do it regularly, it is quite a challenge by the time I get around to it, and there are lots of levels of clean to aim for. I play with getting the stove to look as if it were brand new by the time I'm finished.

I use a scrubber which is abrasive enough to get the caked food off if I rub hard enough with baking soda, but not so abrasive that I scratch the finish. I take off the burner elements and the pans underneath, even the knobs, and soak them in the sink, to be tackled at the end. Then I scrub every square inch of stove surface, favoring a circular motion at times, at others, a back and forth. It all depends on the location and topology of the crud. I get into the round and round or the back and forth, feeling the motion in my whole body, no longer trying to clean the stove so it will look nice, only moving, moving, watching, watching as things change slowly before my eyes. At the end, I wipe the surfaces carefully with a damp sponge.

Music adds to the experience at times. Other times, I prefer silence for my work. One Saturday morning, a tape by Bobby McFerrin was playing in the cassette player when the occasion arose to clean the stove. So cleaning became dancing, the incantations, sounds, and rhythms and the movements of my body merging, blending together, sounds unfolding with motion, sensations in my arm aplenty, modulations in finger pressure on the scrubber as required, caked remains of former cookings slowly changing form and disappearing, all rising and falling in awareness with the music. One big dance of presence, a celebration of now. And, at the end, a clean stove. The voice inside that ordinarily claims credit for such things ("See how clean I got the stove") and seeks approval for it ("Didn't I do a good job?") stirs, but is quickly held in a larger understanding of what had transpired.

Mindfully speaking, I can't get away with claiming that "I" cleaned the stove. It's more like the stove cleaned itself, with the help of Bobby McFerrin, the scrubber, the baking soda, and the sponge, with guest appearances by hot water and a string of present moments.

What Is My Job on the Planet with a Capital J?

"What is my job on the planet?" is one question we might do well to ask ourselves over and over again. Otherwise, we may wind up doing somebody else's job and not even know it. And what's more, that somebody else might be a figment of our own imagination and maybe a prisoner of it as well.

As thinking creatures, packaged, as are all life forms, in unique organismic units we call bodies, and simultaneously totally and impersonally embedded in the warp and woof of life's ceaseless unfolding, we have a singular capacity to take responsibility for our unique piece of what it means to be alive, at least while we have our brief moment in the sun. But we also have the singular capacity of letting our thinking mind entirely cloud our transit through this world. We are at risk of never realizing our uniqueness—at least as long as we remain in the shadow cast by our thought habits and conditioning.

Buckminster Fuller, the discoverer/inventor of the geodesic dome, at age thirty-two contemplated suicide for a few hours one night at the edge of Lake Michigan, as the story goes, after a series of business failures that left him feeling he had made such a mess of his life that the best move would be for him to remove himself from the scene and make things simpler for his wife and infant daughter. Apparently everything he had touched or undertaken had turned to dust in spite of his incredible creativity and imagination, which were only recognized later. However, instead of ending his life, Fuller decided (perhaps because of his deep conviction in the underlying unity and order of the universe, of which he knew himself to be an integral part) to live from then on *as if* he had died that night.

Being dead, he wouldn't have to worry about how things worked out any longer for himself personally and would be free to devote himself to living as a representative of the universe. The rest of his life would be a gift. Instead of living for himself, he would devote himself to asking, "What is it on this planet [which he referred to as Spaceship Earth] that needs doing that I know something about, that probably won't happen unless I take responsibility for it?" He decided he would just ask that question continuously and do what came to him, following his nose. In this way, working for humanity as an employee of the universe at large, you get to modify and contribute to your locale by who you are, how you are, and what you do. But it's no longer personal. It's just part of the totality of the universe expressing itself.

Rarely do we question and then contemplate with determination what our hearts are calling us to do and to be. I like to frame such efforts in question form: "What is my job on the planet with a capital J?", or, "What do I care about so much that I would pay to do it?" If I ask such a question and I don't come up with an answer, other than, "I don't know," then I just keep asking the question. If you start reflecting on such questions when you're in your twenties, by the time you are thirty-five or forty, or fifty or sixty, the inquiry itself may have led you a few places that you would not have gone had you merely followed mainstream conventions, or your parents' expectations for you, or even worse, your own unexamined self-limiting beliefs and expectations.

You can start asking this question any time, at any age. There is never a time of life when it would not have a profound effect on your view of things and the choices you make. It may not mean that you will change *what* you do, but it may mean that you may want to change how you see it or hold it, and perhaps *how* you do it. Once the universe is your employer, very interesting things start to happen, even if someone else is cutting your paycheck. But you do have to be patient. It takes time to grow this way of being in your life. The place to start of course is right here. The best time? How about now?

You never know what will come of such introspections. Fuller himself was fond of stating that what seems to be happening at the moment is never the full story of what is really going on. He liked to point out that for the honey bee, it is the honey that is important. But the bee is at the same time nature's vehicle for carrying out cross-pollination of the flowers. Interconnectedness is a fundamental principle of nature. Nothing is isolated. Each event connects with others. Things are constantly unfolding on different levels. It's for us to perceive the warp and woof of it all as best we can and learn to follow our own threads through the tapestry of life with authenticity and resolve.

Fuller believed in an underlying architecture of nature, in which form and function were inextricably linked. He believed that nature's blueprints would make sense and would have practical relevance to our lives on many levels. Before he died, X-ray crystallographic studies had demonstrated that many viruses—submicroscopic assemblies of macromolecules on the edge of life itself—are structured along the same geodesic principles as those he discovered by playing around with polyhedra.

He didn't live long enough to see it, but in addition to all his other seminal inventions and ideas, a whole new field of chemistry opened up around the unpredicted discovery of soccer ball–like carbon compounds with remarkable properties which quickly became known as Buckminsterfullerenes or buckyballs. Playing in his sandbox, following his own path, his musings led to discoveries and worlds he never dreamed of. So can yours. Fuller never thought of himself as special in any sense, just a regular person who liked to play with ideas and with forms. His motto was: "If I can understand it, anybody can understand it."

*

Insist on yourself; never imitate. Your own gift you can present every moment with the cumulative force of a whole life's cultivation; but of the adopted talent of another you have only an extemporaneous half possession. . . . Do that which is assigned to you, and you cannot hope too much or dare too much.

RALPH WALDO EMERSON, *Self-Reliance*

Mount Analogue

"He may. But in the end, it's the mountain that will decide who will climb it."

EVEREST CLIMB LEADER when asked whether an older veteran climber would get a chance at the summit

There are outer mountains and inner mountains. Their very presence beckons to us, calls us to ascend. Perhaps the full teaching of a mountain is that you carry the whole mountain inside yourself, the outer one as well as the inner. And sometimes you search and search for the mountain without finding it until the time comes when you are sufficiently motivated and prepared to find a way through, first to the base, then to the summit. The mountain climb is a powerful metaphor for the life quest, the spiritual journey, the path of growth, transformation, and understanding. The arduous difficulties we encounter along the way embody the very challenges we need in order to stretch ourselves and thereby expand our boundaries. In the end, it is life itself which is the mountain, the teacher, serving us up perfect opportunities to do the inner work of growing in strength and wisdom. And we have a lot of learning and growing to do once we choose to make the journey. The risks are considerable, the sacrifices awesome, the outcome always uncertain. Ultimately, it is the climb itself which is the adventure, not just standing at the top.

First we learn what it's like at the base. Only later do we encounter the slopes, and finally, perhaps, the top. But you can't stay at the top of a mountain. The journey up is not complete without the descent, the stepping back and seeing the whole again from afar. Having been at the summit, however, you have gained a new perspective, and it may change your way of seeing forever.

In a wonderfully unfinished story called "Mount Analogue," René Daumal once mapped a piece of this inward adventure. The part I remember most vividly involves the rule on Mount Analogue that before you move up the mountain to your next encampment, you must replenish the camp you are leaving for those who will come after you, and go down the mountain a ways to share with the other climbers your knowledge from farther up so that they may have some benefit from what you have learned so far on your own ascent.

In a way, that's all any of us do when we teach. As best we can, we show others what we have seen up to now. It's at best a progress report, a map of our experiences, by no means the absolute truth. And so the adventure unfolds. We are all on Mount Analogue together. And we need each other's help.

Interconnectedness

It seems we know full well from childhood that everything is connected to everything else in certain ways, that this happens because that happened, that for this to happen, that has to happen. Just recall all those old folk tales, such as the one about the fox who drinks most of an old woman's pail of milk which she neglected to watch as she was gathering wood for a fire. She cuts off his tail in a fit of anger. The fox asks for his tail back, and the old woman says she will sew his tail back on for him if he will give her back her milk. So he goes to the cow in the field and asks for some milk, and the cow says she will give the fox some milk if the fox brings her some grass. So the fox goes to the field and asks for some grass, and the field says, "Bring me some water." So he goes to the stream and asks for water and the stream says, "Bring me a jug." This goes on until a miller, out of kindness and sympathy, gives the fox some grain to give the hen to get the egg to give to the peddler to get the bead to give to the maiden to get the jug to fetch the water ... and so the fox gets his tail back and goes away happy. This has to happen in order for that to happen. Nothing comes from nothing. Everything has antecedents. Even the miller's kindness came from somewhere.

Looking deeply into any process, we can see that the same applies. No sunlight, no life. No water, no life. No plants, no photosynthesis, no photosynthesis, no oxygen for animals to breathe. No parents, no you. No trucks, no food in the cities. No truck manufacturers, no trucks. No steel workers, no steel for the manufacturers. No mining, no steel for the steel workers. No food, no steel workers. No rain, no food. No sunlight, no rain. No conditions for star and planet formation in the formative universe, no sunlight, no Earth. These relationships are not always simple and linear. Usually things are embedded in a complex web of finely balanced interconnections. Certainly what we call life, or health, or the biosphere, are all complex systems of interconnections, with no absolute starting point or end point.

So we see the futility and the danger of letting our thinking make any thing or circumstance into an absolutely separate existence without being mindful of interconnectedness and flux. Everything is related to everything else and, in a way, simultaneously contains everything else and is contained by everything else. What is more, everything is in flux. Stars are born, go through stages, and die. Planets also have a rhythm of formation and ultimate demise. New cars are already on their way to the junk heap even before they leave the factory. This awareness might truly enhance our appreciation of impermanence and help us to take things and circumstances and relationships less for granted while they are around. We might appreciate life more, people more, food more, opinions more, moments more, if we perceive, by our own looking more deeply into them, that everything we are in contact with connects us to the whole world in each moment, and that things and other people, and even places and circumstances, are only here temporarily. It makes now so much more interesting. In fact, it makes now everything.

Mindfulness of breathing is one string on which the beads of our experience, our thoughts, our feelings, our emotions, our perceptions, our impulses, our understanding, our very consciousness can be threaded. The necklace created is something new—not a thing really, but a new way of seeing, a new way of being, a new way of experiencing that permits a new way of acting in the world. This new way seems to connect what seems to be isolated. But actually, nothing is ever isolated and needs reconnecting. It's our way of seeing which creates and maintains separation.

This new way of seeing and new way of being holds life fragments and gives them place. It honors each moment in its own fullness within a larger fullness. Mindfulness practice is simply the ongoing discovery of the thread of interconnectedness. At some point, we may even come to see that it is not quite correct to say that we are doing the threading. It's more like we become conscious of a connectedness which has been here all the time. We have climbed to a vantagepoint from which we can more readily perceive wholeness, and can cradle the flow of present moments in awareness. The flow of the breath and the flow of present moments interpenetrate, beads and thread together giving something larger.

*

One merges into another, groups melt into ecological groups until the time when what we know as life meets and enters what we think of as non-life: barnacle and rock, rock and earth, earth and tree, tree and rain and air. . . . And it is a strange thing that most of the feeling we call religious, most of the mystical outcrying which is one of the most prized and used and desired reactions of our species, is really the understanding and the attempt to say that man is related to the whole thing, related inextricably to all reality, known and unknowable. This is a simple thing to say, but the profound feeling of it made a Jesus, a St. Augustine, a St. Francis, a Roger Bacon, a Charles Darwin, and an Einstein. Each of them in his own tempo and with his own voice discovered and reaffirmed with astonishment the knowledge that all things are one thing and that one thing is all things—plankton, a shimmering phosphorescence on the sea and spinning planets and the expanding universe, all bound together by the elastic string of time.

JOHN STEINBECK AND
EDWARD F. RICKETTS,
Sea of Cortez

Non-Harming—Ahimsa

A friend came back after several years in Nepal and India in 1973 and said of himself, "If I can't do anything useful, at least I would like to do as little harm as possible."

I guess you can bring back all sorts of communicable things from distant parts if you're not careful. I was infected with the idea of *ahimsa* right then and there in my living room, and I have never forgotten the moment it happened. I had heard it before. The attitude of non-harming lies at the heart of yoga practice and of the Hippocratic Oath. It was the underlying principle of Gandhi's revolution and of his personal meditation practice. But there was something about the sincerity with which my friend made his comment, coupled with the incongruity of the person I thought I knew saying it, that impressed me. It struck me as a good way to relate to the world and to oneself. Why *not* try to live so as to cause as little damage and suffering as possible? If we lived that way, we wouldn't have the insane levels of violence that dominate our lives and our thinking today. And we would be more generous toward ourselves as well, on the meditation cushion, and off it.

Like any other view, non-harming may be a terrific principle, but it's the living of it that counts. You can start practicing *ahimsa*'s gentleness on yourself and in your life with others in any moment.

Do you sometimes find that you are hard on yourself and put yourself down? Remember *ahimsa* in that moment. See it and let it go.

Do you talk about others behind their backs? *Ahimsa.*

Do you push yourself beyond your limits with no regard for your body and your well-being? *Ahimsa.*

Do you cause other people pain or grief? *Ahimsa.* It is easy to relate with *ahimsa* to someone who doesn't threaten you. The test is in how you will relate to a person or situation when you do feel threatened.

The willingness to harm or hurt comes ultimately out of fear. Non-harming requires that you see your own fears and that you understand them and own them. Owning them means taking responsibility for them. Taking responsibility means not letting fear completely dictate your vision or your view. Only mindfulness of our own clinging and rejecting, and a willingness to grapple with these mind states, however painful the encounter, can free us from this circle of suffering. Without a daily embodiment in practice, lofty ideals tend to succumb to self-interest.

*

Ahimsa is the attribute of the soul, and therefore,
to be practiced by everybody in all the affairs of life.
If it cannot be practiced in all departments, it has
no practical value.

MAHATMA GANDHI

✻

If you can't love King George V, say, or Sir Winston
Churchill, start with your wife, or your husband, or
your children. Try to put their welfare first and your
own last every minute of the day, and let the circle of
your love expand from there. As long as you are trying
your very best, there can be no question of failure.

MAHATMA GANDHI

Karma

I've heard Zen masters say that daily meditation practice could turn bad karma into good karma. I always chalked this up to a quaint moralistic sales pitch. It took me years to get the point. I guess that's my karma.

Karma means that this happens because that happened. B is connected in some way to A, every effect has an antecedent cause, and every cause an effect that is its measure and its consequence, at least at the non-quantum level. Overall, when we speak of a person's karma, it means the sum total of the person's direction in life and the tenor of the things that occur around that person, caused by antecedent conditions, actions, thoughts, feelings, sense impressions, desires. Karma is often wrongly confused with the notion of a fixed destiny. It is more like an accumulation of tendencies that can lock us into particular behavior patterns, which themselves result in further accumulations of tendencies of a similar nature. So, it is easy to become imprisoned by our karma and to think that the cause always lies elsewhere—with other people and conditions beyond our control, never within ourselves. But it is not necessary to be a prisoner of old karma. It is always possible to change your karma. You can make new karma. But there is only one time that you ever have to do it in. Can you guess when that might be?

Here's how mindfulness changes karma. When you sit, you are not allowing your impulses to translate into action. For the time being, at least, you are just watching them. Looking at them, you quickly see that all impulses in the mind arise and pass away, that they have a life of their own, that they are not you but just thinking, and that you do not have to be ruled by them. Not feeding or reacting to impulses, you come to understand their nature as thoughts directly. This process actually burns up destructive impulses in the fires of concentration and equanimity and non-doing. At the same time, creative insights and creative impulses are no longer squeezed out so much by the more turbulent, destructive ones. They are nourished as they are perceived and held in awareness. Mindfulness can thereby re-fashion the links in the chain of actions and consequences, and in doing so it unchains us, frees us, and opens up new directions for us through the moments we call life. Without mindfulness, we are all too easily stuck in the momentum coming out of the past, with no clue to our own imprisonment, and no way out. Our dilemma always seems to be the other person's fault, or the world's fault, so our own views and feelings are always justified. The present moment is never a new beginning because we keep it from becoming one.

How else to explain, for example, the all-too-common observation that two people who have lived their whole adult lives together, had children together, tasted success in their own realms to a degree not usually achieved, might in their later years, when by all accounts they should be enjoying the fruits of their labors, each blame the other for making life miserable, for feeling isolated, trapped in a bad dream, so mistreated and abused that anger and hurt are the fabric of each day? Karma. In one form or another, you see it over and over again in relationships gone sour or missing something fundamental from the start, the absence of which invites sadness, bitterness, hurt. Sooner or later, we are most likely to reap that which we have sown. Practice anger and isolation in a relationship for forty years, and you wind up imprisoned in anger and isolation. No big surprise. And it is hardly satisfactory to apportion blame here.

Ultimately, it is our mindlessness that imprisons us. We get better and better at being out of touch with the full range of our possibilities, and more and more stuck in our cultivated-over-a-lifetime habits of not-seeing, but only reacting and blaming.

Working in prisons, I get to see the results of "bad" karma up close, although it's hardly any different outside the prison walls. Every inmate has a story of one thing leading to another. After all, that's what stories are. One thing leading to another. Many hardly know what happened to them, what went wrong. Usually it's a long chain of events starting with parents and family, the culture of the streets, poverty and violence, trusting people you shouldn't, looking for an easy buck, soothing the hurt and dulling the senses with alcohol and other chemicals which cloud mind and body. Drugs do it, but so do history, deprivation, and arrested development. They warp thoughts and feelings, actions and values, leaving few avenues for modulating or even recognizing hurtful, cruel, destructive and self-destructive impulses or cravings.

And so, in one moment, which all your other moments led up to, unbeknownst to you, you can "lose your mind," commit an irreversible act, and then experience the myriad ways in which it shapes future moments. Everything has consequences, whether we know it or not, whether we are "caught" by the police or not. We are always caught. Caught in the karma of it. We build our own prisons every day. In one way, my friends in prison made their choices, whether they knew it or not. In other ways, they didn't have choices. They never knew choices were there. Once again, we encounter what Buddhists call "unawareness," or ignorance. It is ignorance of how unexamined impulses, especially those colored by greed or hatred, however justified, rationalized, or legal, can warp one's mind and one's life. Such mind states affect us all, sometimes in big dramatic ways, but most often by more subtle paths. We can all be imprisoned by incessant wanting, by a mind clouded with ideas and opinions it clings to as if they were truths.

If we hope to change our karma, it means we have to stop making those things happen that cloud mind and body and color our every action. It doesn't mean doing good deeds. It means knowing who you are and that you are not your karma, whatever it may be at this moment. It means aligning yourself with the way things actually are. It means seeing clearly.

Where to start? Why not with your own mind? After all, it is the instrument through which all your thoughts and feelings, impulses and perceptions are translated into actions in the world. When you stop outward activity for some time and practice being still, right there, in that moment, with that decision to sit, you are already breaking the flow of old karma and creating an entirely new and healthier karma. Herein lies the root of change, the turning point of a life lived.

The very act of stopping, of nurturing moments of nondoing, of simply watching, puts you on an entirely different footing vis-à-vis the future. How? Because it is only by being fully in this moment that any future moment might be one of greater understanding, clarity, and kindness, one less dominated by fear or hurt and more by dignity and acceptance. Only what happens now happens later. If there is no mindfulness or equanimity or compassion now, in the only time we ever have to contact it and nourish ourselves, how likely is it that it will magically appear later, under stress or duress?

*

The idea that the soul will join with the ecstatic

just because the body is rotten—

that is all fantasy.

What is found now is found then.

KABIR

Wholeness and Oneness

When we are in touch with being whole, we feel at one with everything. When we feel at one with everything, we feel whole ourselves.

Sitting still or lying still, in any moment we can reconnect with our body, transcend the body, merge with the breath, with the universe, experience ourselves as whole and folded into larger and larger wholes. A taste of interconnectedness brings deep knowledge of belonging, a sense of being an intimate part of things, a sense of being at home wherever we are. We may taste and wonder at an ancient timelessness beyond birth and death, and simultaneously experience the fleeting brevity of this life as we pass through it, the impermanence of our ties to our body, to this moment, to each other. Knowing our wholeness directly in the meditation practice, we may find ourselves coming to terms with things as they are, a deepening of understanding and compassion, a lessening of anguish and despair.

Wholeness is the root of everything that the words *health*, *healing*, and *holy* signify in our language and our culture.

When we perceive our intrinsic wholeness, there is truly no place to go and nothing to do. Thus, we are free to choose a path for ourselves. Stillness becomes available in doing and in non-doing. We find it lying within ourselves at all times, and as we touch it, taste it, listen to it, the body cannot but touch it, taste it, listen as well, and in so doing, let go. And the mind too comes to listen, and knows at least a moment of peace. Open and receptive, we find balance and harmony right here, all space folded into this place, all moments folded into this moment.

*

Ordinary men hate solitude.
But the Master makes use of it,
embracing his aloneness, realizing
he is one with the whole universe

LAO-TZU, *Tao-te-Ching*

*

Peace comes within the souls of men
When they realize their oneness with the universe.

BLACK ELK

Siddhartha listened. He was now listening intently, completely absorbed, quite empty, taking in everything. He felt that he had now completely learned the art of listening. He had often heard all this before, all these numerous voices in the river, but today they sounded different. He could no longer distinguish the different voices—the merry voice from the weeping voice, the childish voice from the manly voice. They all belonged to each other: the lament of those who yearn, the laughter of the wise, the cry of indignation and the groan of the dying. They were all interwoven and interlocked, entwined in a thousand ways. And all the voices, all the goals, all the pleasures, all the good and evil, all of them together was the world. All of them together was the stream of events, the music of life. When Siddhartha listened attentively to this river, to this song of a thousand voices, when he did not listen to the sorrow or the laughter, when he did not bind his soul to any one particular voice and absorb it in his Self, but heard them all, the whole, the unity, then the great song of a thousand voices consisted of one word.

HERMANN HESSE, *Siddhartha*

*

What is needed is to learn afresh, to observe, and to discover for ourselves, the meaning of wholeness.

DAVID BOHM, *Wholeness and the Implicate Order*

*

I am large; I contain multitudes.

WALT WHITMAN, *Leaves of Grass*

Eachness and Suchness

Wholeness experienced first hand cannot be tyrannical, for it is infinite in its diversity and finds itself mirrored and embedded in each particular, like the Hindu goddess Indra's net, a symbol of the universe, which has jewels at all the vertices, each one capturing the reflections of the entire net and so containing the whole. Some would have us worship, uniformly, at the altar of oneness, using the *idea* of unity rather than an ongoing encounter with it to steamroller-like, flatten out all differences. But it is in the unique qualities of this and that, their particular individuality and properties—in their eachness and their suchness, if you will—that all poetry and art, science and life, wonder, grace, and richness reside.

All faces resemble each other, yet how easily we see in each uniqueness, individuality, an identity. How deeply we value these differences. The ocean is a whole, but it has countless waves, every one different from all the others; it has currents, each unique, ever-changing; the bottom is a landscape all its own, different everywhere; similarly the shoreline. The atmosphere is whole, but its currents have unique signatures, even though they are just wind. Life on earth is a whole, yet it expresses itself in unique time-bound bodies, microscopic or visible, plant or animal, extinct or living. So there can be no one place to be. There can be no one way to be, no one way to practice, no one way to learn, no one way to love, no one way to grow or to heal, no one way to live, no one way to feel, no one thing to know or be known. The particulars count.

✷

The Chicadee
The chicadee
Hops near to me.

THOREAU

✷

The man pulling radishes
pointed the way
with a radish.

ISSA

✷

Old pond,
frog jumps in—
splash.

BASHO

✷

Midnight. No waves,
no wind, the empty boat
is flooded with moonlight.

DOGEN

Get the idea?

Selfing

The true value of a human being is determined primarily by the measure and sense in which he has attained liberation from the self.

ALBERT EINSTEIN, *The World As I See It*

"I," "me," and "mine" are products of our thinking. My friend Larry Rosenberg, of the Cambridge Insight Meditation Center, calls it "selfing," that inevitable and incorrigible tendency to construct out of almost everything and every situation an "I," a "me," and a "mine," and then to operate in the world from that limited perspective which is mostly fantasy and defense. Hardly a moment passes that this doesn't happen, but it is so much a part of the fabric of our world that it goes completely unnoticed, much as the proverbial fish has no knowledge of water, so thoroughly is it immersed in it. You can see this for yourself easily enough whether you are meditating in silence or just living a five-minute segment of your life. Out of virtually any and every moment and experience, our thinking mind constructs "my" moment, "my" experience, "my" child, "my" hunger, "my" desire, "my" opinion, "my" way, "my" authority, "my" future, "my" knowledge, "my" body, "my" mind, "my" house, "my" land, "my" idea, "my" feelings, "my" car, "my" problem.

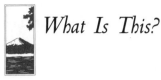

What Is This?

The spirit of inquiry is fundamental to living mindfully. Inquiry is not just a way to solve problems. It is a way to make sure you are staying in touch with the basic mystery of life itself and of our presence here. Who am I? Where am I going? What does it mean to be? What does it mean to be a . . . man, woman, child, parent; a student, a worker, a boss, an inmate; a homeless person? What is my karma? Where am I now? What is my way? What is my job on the planet with a capital J?

Inquiry doesn't mean looking for answers, especially quick answers which come out of superficial thinking. It means asking without expecting answers, just pondering the question, carrying the wondering with you, letting it percolate, bubble, cook, ripen, come in and out of awareness, just as everything else comes in and out of awareness.

You don't have to be still to inquire. Inquiry and mindfulness can occur simultaneously in the unfolding of your daily life. In fact, inquiry and mindfulness are one and the same thing, come to from different directions. You can ponder "What am I" or "What is this?" or "Where am I going?" or "What is my job?" as you are fixing a car, walking to work, doing the dishes, listening to your daughter sing on a starlit spring evening, or looking for a job.

Problems of all shapes and sizes come up all the time in life. They range from the trivial to the profound to the overwhelming. The challenge here is to meet them with inquiry, in the spirit of mindfulness. It would mean asking, "What is this thought, this feeling, this dilemma?" "How am I going to deal with it?" Or even, "Am I willing to deal with it or even acknowledge it?"

The first step is to acknowledge that there *is* a problem, which means there is strain or tension or disharmony of some kind. It might take us forty or fifty years to even come close to acknowledging some of the big demons we carry. But maybe that's okay too. There's no timetable for inquiry. It's like a pot sitting on your shelf. It's ready to do the cooking whenever you are ready to take it down, put something in it, and heat it on the stove.

Inquiry means asking questions, over and over again. Do we have the courage to look at something, whatever it is, and to inquire, what is this? What is going on? It involves looking deeply for a sustained period, questioning, questioning, what is this? What is wrong? What is at the root of the problem? What is the evidence? What are the connections? What would a happy solution look like? Questioning, questioning, continually questioning.

Inquiry is not so much thinking about answers, although the questioning will produce a lot of thoughts that look like answers. It really involves just listening to the thinking that your questioning evokes, as if you were sitting by the side of stream of your own thoughts, listening to the water flow o and around the rocks, listening, listening, and watching occasional leaf or twig as it is carried along.

If you observe this process of selfing with sustained attention and inquiry, you will see that what we call "the self" is really a construct of our own mind, and hardly a permanent one, either. If you look deeply for a stable, indivisible self, for the core "you" that underlies "your" experience, you are not likely to find it other than in more thinking. You might say you are your name, but that is not quite accurate. Your name is just a label. The same is true of your age, your gender, your opinions, and so on. None are fundamental to who you are.

When you inquire in this way as deeply as you can follow the thread into who you are or what you are, you are almost sure to find that there is no solid place to land. If you ask: "Who is the I who is asking who am I?", ultimately you come to, "I don't know." The "I" just appears as a construct which is known by its attributes, none of which, taken singly or together, really makes up the whole of the person. Moreover, the "I" construct has the tendency continually to dissolve and reconstruct itself, virtually moment by moment. It also has a strong tendency to feel diminished, small, insecure, and uncertain, since its existence is so tenuous to begin with. This only makes the tyranny and suffering associated with unawareness of how much we are caught up in "I," "me," and "mine" that much worse.

Then there is the problem of outside forces. The "I" tends to feel good when outside circumstances are supporting its belief in its own goodness, and bad when it runs into criticism, difficulties, and what it perceives as obstacles and defeats. Here perhaps lies a major explanation for diminished self-esteem in many people. We aren't really familiar with this constructed aspect of our identity process. This makes it easy for us to lose our balance and feel vulnerable and inconsequential when we are not propped up and reinforced in our need for approval or for feeling important. We are likely to continually seek interior stability through outside rewards, through material possessions, and from others who love us. In this way, we keep our self-construct going. Yet in spite of all this self-generating activity, there may still be no sense of enduring stability in one's own being, nor calmness in the mind. Buddhists might say that this is because there is no absolute separate "self" in the first place, just the process of continual self-construction or "selfing." If we could only recognize the process of selfing as an ingrained habit and then give ourselves permission to take the day off, to stop trying so hard to be "somebody" and instead just experience being, perhaps we would be a lot happier and more relaxed.

This doesn't mean, by the way, that "you have to be a somebody before you can be a nobody," one of the big New Age distortions of meditation practice, by which is meant that you should have a robust sense of self before you explore the emptiness of "no-self." No-self does not mean being a nobody. What it means is that everything is interdependent and that there is no isolated, independent core "you." You are only you in relationship to all other forces and events in the world—including your parents, your childhood, your thoughts and feelings, outside events, time, and so on. Moreover, you are already a somebody, no matter what. You are who you already are. But who you are is not your name, your age, your childhood, your beliefs, your fears. They are part of it, but not the whole.

So, when we speak about not trying so hard to be "somebody" and instead just experience being, directly, what it means is that you start from where you find yourself and work here. Meditation is not about trying to become a nobody, or a contemplative zombie, incapable of living in the real world and facing real problems. It's about seeing things as they are, without the distortions of our own thought processes. Part of that is perceiving that everything is interconnected and that while our conventional sense of "having" a self is helpful in many ways, it is not absolutely real or solid or permanent. So, if you stop trying to make yourself into more than you are out of fear that you are less than you are, whoever you really are will be a lot lighter and happier, and easier to live with, too.

We might begin by taking things a little less personally. When something happens, try to see it without the self-orientation, just for fun. Maybe it just happened. Maybe it's not aimed at you. Watch your mind at such times. Is it getting into "I" this and "me" that? Ask yourself, "Who am I?" or, "What is this 'I' that is claiming ownership?"

Awareness itself can help balance out the selfing and reduce its impact. Notice, too, that the self is impermanent. Whatever you try to hold on to that has to do with yourself eludes you. It can't be held because it is constantly changing, decaying, and being reconstructed again, always slightly differently, depending on the circumstances of the moment. This makes the sense of self what is called in chaos theory a "strange attractor," a pattern which embodies order, yet is also unpredictably disordered. It never repeats itself. Whenever you look, it is slightly different.

The elusive nature of a concrete, permanent, unchanging self is quite a hopeful observation. It means that you can stop taking yourself so damn seriously and get out from under the pressures of having the details of your personal life be central to the operating of the universe. By recognizing and letting go of selfing impulses, we accord the universe a little more room to make things happen. Since we are folded into the universe and participate in its unfolding, it will defer in the face of too much self-centered, self-indulgent, self-critical, self-insecure, self-anxious activity on our part, and arrange for the dream world of our self-oriented thinking to look and feel only too real.

Anger

The look of utter despair and silent pleading for me not to get angry etched into my daughter Naushon's 11-year-old face as I am getting out of the car at her friend's house early one Sunday morning does penetrate my awareness, but not completely enough to rein in the annoyance and anger which she sees rising in me, and which she fears will make a scene and embarrass her. I am feeling too much momentum in this moment to stop completely, although later I would wish I had. I wished that I had let her look stop me in that moment, touch me, turn me toward seeing what was really important—namely, that she feels she can depend on me and trust me rather than fear that I will betray her or mortify her emerging social sensitivity. But I am too upset in this moment about being manipulated by her friend, who was supposed to be ready at a certain time and isn't, to fully appreciate my daughter's problem here.

I am caught up in an eddy of self-righteous indignation. My "I" does not want to be kept waiting, to be taken advantage of. I reassure her that I will not make a scene, but that I also want to communicate about it right now because I am feeling used. I make early morning inquiries, tinged with annoyance, of her sleepy mother; then wait, inwardly fuming, for what turns out to be a remarkably short time.

And so the matter dissolved. But not in my memory, which still carries, and I hope always will, that look on my daughter's face that I was unable to read quickly enough to be fully present for. Had I been able to, the anger would have died then and there.

There is a price we pay for being attached to a narrow view of being "right." My passing mood state is far less important to me than her trust. But in that moment, her trust got trampled all the same. Without care and awareness, small-minded feeling states can dominate the moment. It happens all the time. The collective pain we cause others and ourselves bleeds our souls. Hard as it is for us to admit, especially about ourselves, self-tinged anger may be something we indulge in and surrender to far too often.

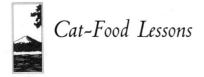

Cat-Food Lessons

I hate finding caked cat dishes in the kitchen sink along with ours. I'm not sure why this pushes my buttons so strongly, but it does. Perhaps it comes from not having had a pet when I was growing up. Or maybe I think it's a public health threat (you know, viruses and the like). When I choose to clean the cats' bowls, I first clean the whole sink of our dishes, then I wash theirs. Anyway, I don't like it when I find dirty cat dishes in the sink, and I react right away when I do.

First I get angry. Then the anger gets more personal and I find myself directing it at whoever I think is the culprit, which is usually my wife, Myla. I feel hurt because she doesn't respect my feelings. I tell her on countless occasions that I don't like it, that it disgusts me. I've asked her as politely as I know how not do it, but she often does it anyway. She feels I'm being silly and compulsive, and when she's pressed for time, she just leaves the caked cat dishes soaking in the sink.

My discovery of cat food in the sink can quickly escalate to a heated dispute, mostly because I am feeling angry and hurt and above all justified in "my" anger, "my" hurt, because I know "I" am right. Cat food shouldn't be in the sink! But when it is, the selfing on my part can get rather strong.

Recently, I've noticed that I am not getting so bent out of

shape about this. I didn't specifically try to change how I'm dealing with it. I still feel the same about the cat food, but somehow, I'm seeing the whole thing differently too, with greater awareness and with much more of a sense of humor. For one, when it happens now—and it still does with annoying frequency—I find that I am aware of my reaction the moment it happens and I look at it. "This is it," I remind myself!

I observe the anger as it starts rising in me. It turns out that it is preceded by a mild feeling of revulsion. Then I notice the stirrings of a feeling of betrayal which is not so mild. Someone in my family didn't respect *my* request, and *I* am taking it very personally. After all, my feelings count in the family, don't they?

I have taken to experimenting with my reactions at the kitchen sink by watching them very closely without acting on them. I can report that the initial feeling of revulsion is not all that bad, and if I stay with it, breathe with it, and permit myself to just feel it, it actually goes away within a second or two. I have also noticed that it is the sense of betrayal, of being thwarted in my wishes, that makes me mad much more than the cat food itself. So, I discover, it's not really the cat food by itself that is the source of my anger. It's that I'm not feeling listened to and respected. Very different from the cat food. Aha!

Then I remember that my wife and kids see this whole thing very differently. They think I am making a big deal out of nothing, and that while they will try to respect my wishes when it feels reasonable to them, at other times it doesn't and they just do it anyway, maybe even without thinking about me at all.

So I've stopped taking it personally. When I really don't want cat food in the sink, I roll up my sleeves and I clean the dishes in that moment. Otherwise, I just leave them there and go away. We no longer have fights about it. In fact, I find myself smiling now when I do come across the offending objects in the sink. After all, they have taught me a lot.

TRY: Watching your reactions in situations that annoy you or make you angry. Notice how even speaking of something "making" you angry surrenders your power to others. Such occasions are good opportunities to experiment with mindfulness as a pot into which you can put all your feelings and just be with them, letting them slowly cook, reminding yourself that you don't have to do anything with them right away, that they will become more cooked, more easily digested and understood simply by holding them in the pot of mindfulness.

Observe the ways in which your feelings are creations of your mind's view of things, and that maybe that view is not complete. Can you allow this state of affairs to be okay and neither make

yourself right or wrong? Can you be patient enough and coura-
geous enough to explore putting stronger and stronger emotions
into the pot and just holding them and letting them cook, rather
than projecting them outward and forcing the world to be as
you want it to be now? Can you see how this practice might lead
to knowing yourself in new ways, and freeing yourself from old,
worn-out, limiting views?

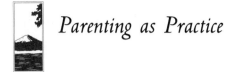

Parenting as Practice

I took up meditating when I was in my early twenties. In those days, I had some flexibility in terms of my time, and was able to periodically attend meditation retreats lasting ten days or two weeks. These retreats were designed so that the participants could devote each day from early morning to late at night solely to mindful sitting and walking, with a few hearty vegetarian meals thrown in, all in silence. We were supported in this inner work by excellent meditation teachers, who would give inspiring talks in the evening to help us deepen and broaden our practice, and who would see us every so often for individual interviews to check on how things were going.

I loved these retreats because they enabled me to put everything else in my life on hold, go off someplace pleasant and peaceful in the countryside, get taken care of, and live an extremely simplified contemplative life, where the only real agenda was to practice, practice, practice.

Not that it was easy, mind you. There was often a lot of physical pain just from sitting still for that many hours, and that was nothing compared to the emotional pain which would sometimes surface as the mind and body became more still and less busy.

When my wife and I decided to have children, I knew that

I would have to give up the retreats, at least for some time. I said to myself that I could always return to the contemplative setting when my children had grown up enough not to need me around all the time. There was a certain romantic touch to the fantasy of returning to the monastic life as an old man. The prospect of giving up these retreats, or at least cutting back on them a lot, didn't bother me too much because, much as I valued them, I had decided that there was a way to look at having children as a meditation retreat in its own right—one that would have most of the important features of those I was giving up, except for the quiet and the simplicity.

This was how I saw it: You could look at each baby as a little Buddha or Zen master, your own private mindfulness teacher, parachuted into your life, whose presence and actions were guaranteed to push every button and challenge every belief and limit you had, giving you continual opportunities to see where you were attached to something and to let go of it. For each child, it would be *at least* an eighteen-year retreat, with virtually no time off for good behavior. The retreat schedule would be relentless and demand continual acts of selflessness and loving kindness. My life, which up to that time basically consisted of looking after my own personal needs and desires, perfectly normal for a young single person, was about to change profoundly. Becoming a parent clearly was going to be the biggest transformation of my adult life so far. To do it well would demand the greatest clarity of view and the greatest letting go and letting be I had ever been challenged with.

For one, babies invite and require attending to constantly. Their needs must be met on their schedule, not yours, and every day, not just when you feel like it. Most importantly, babies and children require your full presence as a being in order to thrive and grow. They need to be held, the more the better, walked with, sung to, rocked, played with, comforted, sometimes nurtured late at night or early in the morning when you are feeling depleted, exhausted, and only want to sleep, or when you have pressing obligations and responsibilities elsewhere. The deep and constantly changing needs of children are all perfect opportunities for parents to be fully present rather than to operate in the automatic pilot mode, to relate consciously rather than mechanically, to sense the being in each child and let his or her vibrancy, vitality, and purity call forth our own. I felt that parenting was nothing short of a perfect opportunity to deepen mindfulness, if I could let the children and the family become my teachers, and remember to recognize and listen carefully to the lessons in living which would be coming fast and furiously.

Like any long retreat, there have been easy periods and harder periods, wonderful moments and deeply painful ones. Through it all, the principle of looking at it as a meditation retreat and honoring the children and the family situation as my teachers has proven its primacy and value time and time again. Parenting is a high pressure job situation. In the early years, it feels like a full-time job for about ten people, and usually there are only two, or even one, to do it all, and no manual which comes with the babies telling you how to proceed. It is the hardest job in the world to do well, and most of the time you don't even know whether you are doing well, or even what that means. And we get virtually no preparation or training for parenting, only on-the-job, moment-to-moment training as things unfold.

At the beginning, there are precious few opportunities for respite. The job calls for you to be continually engaged. And the children are always pushing your limits to find out about the world and about who they are. What's more, as they grow and develop, they change. No sooner have you figured out how to relate well to one situation than they grow out of that and into something you've never seen before. You have to be continually mindful and present so that you aren't lingering with a view of things that no longer applies. And, of course, there are no stock answers or simple formulas for how to do things "right" in the world of parenting. This means you are unavoidably in creative and challenging situations almost all the time, and at the same time, faced with a lot of repetitive tasks which you do over and over, again and again and again.

And it gets more challenging as the children grow older and develop their own ideas and strong wills. It's one thing to look after the needs of babies, which are very simple, after all, especially before they can talk and when they are at their absolute cutest and most adorable. It's quite another to see clearly and to respond effectively and with some modicum of wisdom and balance (after all, *you* are the adult) when there is a continual clash of wills with older children, who are not always so cute and cuddly, who can argue circles around you, tease each other mercilessly, fight, rebel, refuse to listen, get into social situations in which they need your guidance and clarity but may not be open to it; in short, whose needs require a constant energy output that leaves you little time for yourself. The list of situations in which your equanimity and clarity will be sorely challenged and you will find yourself "losing it" is endless. There is simply no escape, no hiding, no dissimilation that will serve either them or you. Your children will see it all from the inside and up close: your foibles, idiosyncrasies, warts and pimples, your shortcomings, your inconsistencies, and your failures.

These trials are not impediments to either parenting or mindfulness practice. They *are* the practice, *if* you can remember to see it this way. Otherwise, your life as a parent can become one very long and unsatisfying burden, in which your lack of strength and clarity of purpose may lead to forgetting to honor or even to see the inner goodness of your children and yourself. Children can easily become wounded and diminished from a childhood which consistently fails to adequately honor their needs and their inner beauty. Wounding will just create more problems for them and for the family, problems with self-confidence and self-esteem, with communication and competencies, problems that don't disappear on their own as the children grow older but usually amplify. And as parents, we may not be open enough to perceive the signs of this diminishment or wounding and then be able to act to heal it because it may have come in some measure through our own hands or through our own lack of awareness. Also, it may be subtle, easily denied, or attributable to other causes, thus freeing us in our own minds from a responsibility which may be truly ours to assume.

It is obvious that, with all that energy going outward, there has to be some source of energy coming in which nurtures and revitalizes the parents from time to time, or the process itself will not be sustainable for long. Where might this energy come from? I can think of only two possible sources: *outside* support from your partner, other family members, friends, baby-sitters, and so on and from doing other things you love, at least occasionally; and *inner* support, which you could get from formal meditation practice if you can make even a little time in your life for stillness, for just being, for just sitting, or for doing a little yoga, for nourishing yourself in ways that you need to be nourished.

I meditate early in the morning because there is no other time when things are quiet in the house and nobody is demanding my attention, and also because, what with work and other obligations, if I don't do it then, I may be too tired or too busy to get to it later. I also find that practicing in the early morning sets the tone for the entire day. It is both a reminder and an affirmation of what is important, and it sets the stage for mindfulness to spill out naturally into other aspects of the day.

But when we had babies in the house, even the morning time was up for grabs. You couldn't be too attached to anything because everything you set out to do, even if you arranged it very carefully, was always getting interrupted or completely thwarted. Our babies slept very little. They always seemed to be up late and to wake up early, especially if I was meditating. They seemed to sense when I was up and would wake up too. Some days I would have to push my time for myself back to 4:00 A.M. to get any sitting or yoga in. At other times I was just too exhausted to care, and figured the sleep was more important anyway. And sometimes I would just sit with the baby on my lap, and let him or her decide how long it would last. They loved being wrapped up in the meditation blanket, with only their heads sticking out, and frequently would stay still for extended periods, while I followed not my breathing but our breathing.

I felt strongly in those days, and still do, that an awareness of my body and my breath and of our close contact as I held them while we sat helped my babies to sense calmness and explore stillness and feelings of acceptance. And their inner relaxation, which was much greater and purer than mine because their minds were not filled with adult thoughts and worries, helped *me* to be more calm and relaxed and present. When they were toddlers, I would do yoga with them climbing up, riding on, or hanging from my body. In playing around on the floor, we would spontaneously discover new yoga postures for two bodies, things that we could do together. A mostly non-verbal, mindful, and respectful body-play of this sort was a source of tremendous fun and joy for me as a father and a deep source of connectedness that we all shared in.

The older children get, the harder it is to remember that they are still live-in Zen masters. The challenges to be mindful and non-reactive, and to look clearly at my reactions and overreactions and to own when I am off seem to get greater as I gradually have less and less direct say in their lives. Old tapes from my own upbringing seem to surface with the volume on full blast before I know what is happening. Archetypal male stuff, about my role in the family, legitimate and illegitimate authority and how to assert my power, how comfortable I feel in the house, interpersonal relationships among people of very different ages and stages and their oft-competing needs. Each day is a new challenge. Often it feels overwhelming, and sometimes quite lonely. You sense widening gulfs, and recognize the importance of distance for healthy psychic development and exploration; but the moving apart, healthy as it may be, also hurts. Sometimes I forget what it means to be an adult myself and get stuck in infantile behaviors. The kids quickly straighten me out and wake me up again if my own mindfulness is not up to the task at that moment.

Parenting and family life can be a perfect field for mindfulness practice, but it's not for the weak-hearted, the selfish or lazy, or the hopelessly romantic. Parenting is a mirror that forces you to look at yourself. If you can learn from what you observe, you just may have a chance to keep growing yourself.

✳

Once the realization is accepted that even between the closest human beings infinite distances continue to exist, a wonderful living side by side can grow up, if they succeed in loving the distance between them which makes it possible for each to see the other whole against the sky.

RAINER MARIA RILKE, *Letters*

✳

The attainment of wholeness requires one to stake one's whole being. Nothing less will do; there can be no easier conditions, no substitutes, no compromises.

C.G. JUNG

TRY: If you are a parent or grandparent, try seeing the children as your teachers. Observe them in silence sometimes. Listen more carefully to them. Read their body language. Assess their self-esteem by watching how they carry themselves, what they draw, what they see, how they behave. What are their needs in this moment? At this time in their day? At this stage in their lives? Ask yourself, "How can I help them right now?" Then follow what your heart tells you. And remember, advice is probably the last thing that will be useful in most situations, unless it is just the right moment for it, and you are very sensitive to the timing and how you frame things. Just being centered yourself, fully present and open and available, is a great gift for them. And mindful hugging doesn't hurt, either.

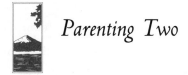

Parenting Two

Of course, you are your children's major life teacher as much as they are your teachers, and how you take on this role will make a big difference in their lives as well as in your own. I see parenting as extended but temporary guardianship. When we think of them as "our" children, or "my" children, and start relating to them as our proper possessions to shape and control to satisfy our own needs, we are, I believe, in deep trouble. Like it or not, children are and will always be their own beings; but they need great love and guidance to come to full humanness. A proper guardian or guide needs wisdom and patience in abundance to pass on what is most important to the generation coming along the path. Some—myself included—need virtually constant mindfulness in addition to our basic instincts for nurturing and loving and kindness in order to do this job well, protecting them as they develop their own strengths, views, and skills for moving along the paths they will later explore more fully on their own.

Some people who find meditation valuable in their own lives are sorely tempted to teach their children to meditate. This could be a big mistake. To my mind, the best way to impart wisdom, meditation, or anything else to your children, especially when they are young, is to live it yourself, embody what you most want to impart, and keep your mouth shut. The more you talk about meditation or extol it or insist that your children do things a certain way, the more likely you are, I think, to turn them off to it for life. They will sense your strong attachment to your view, the aggression behind your dominating them and enforcing certain beliefs that are only your own and not their truth, and they will know that this is not their path but yours. As they grow, they may also detect the hypocrisy of it, as well as any distance between what is being professed and what is being lived.

If you are devoted to your own meditation practice, they will come to know it and see it, and accept it matter of factly, as part of life, a normal activity. They may even sometimes be drawn to imitate you, as they do with most other things parents do. The point is, the motivation to learn meditation and to practice should for the most part originate with them, and be pursued only to the degree that their interest is maintained.

The real teaching is almost entirely non-verbal. My children sometimes do yoga with me because they see me doing it. But most of the time they have more important things to do and no interest in it. The same is true for sitting. But they do know about meditation. They have some idea of what it is, and they know that I value it and practice it myself. And when they want to, they know how to sit from sitting with me when they were little.

If you practice yourself, you will discover certain times when it may be sensible to make meditative recommendations to your children. These suggestions may or may not "work" at the time, but they can be a kind of planting seeds for later. Good occasions are when your children are experiencing pain or fear or are having a hard time letting go into sleep. Without being overbearing or insistent, you can suggest that they tune in to their breathing, slow it down, float on the waves in a little boat, watch the fear or the pain, look for images and colors, use their imagination to "play" with the situation, and then remind themselves that these are just pictures in the mind, like movies; that they can change the movie, the thought, the image, the color, and sometimes feel better quicker and feel more in control.

Sometimes this works well with preschoolers, but they can get embarrassed or think it's silly once they get to be around six or seven. Then this too passes, and they become receptive again at certain times. In any event, seeds have been planted suggesting that there are internal ways to work with fear and pain, and often they will come back to this knowledge when they are older. They will know from direct experience that they are more than just their thoughts and feelings, and can relate to them in ways that give them more choices to participate in and influence the outcomes of various situations; that just because other people's minds are waving about, it doesn't mean that theirs have to too.

Some Pitfalls Along the Path

If you follow the life-long path of mindfulness practice, the biggest potential obstacle at points along your journey will undoubtedly be your thinking mind.

For instance, you might come to think from time to time that you are getting somewhere, especially if you have some satisfying moments that transcend what you have experienced before. Then you might go around thinking, maybe even saying, that you have gotten somewhere, that the meditation practice "works." The ego wants to lay claim and take credit for this special feeling or understanding, whatever it is. As soon as this happens, you are no longer into meditation but into advertising. It is easy to get caught here, using meditation practice to support the self-inflation habit.

As soon as you're caught, you cease seeing clearly. Even a clear insight, once it is claimed by this kind of self-serving thinking, rapidly clouds over and loses its authenticity. So you have to remind yourself that all colorations of "I," "me," and "mine" are just currents of thinking that are liable to carry you away from your own heart and the purity of direct experience. This reminder keeps the practice alive for us at the very moments we may need it the most and are the most ready to betray it. It keeps us looking deeply, in the spirit of inquiry and genuine curiosity, and asking constantly, "What is this?", "What is this?"

Or perhaps, on occasion you may find yourself thinking that you're getting nowhere with your meditation practice. Nothing that you want to happen has happened. There is a sense of staleness, of boredom. Here again, it's the thinking that's the problem. There is nothing wrong with feelings of boredom or staleness, or of not getting anywhere, just as there is nothing wrong with feeling that you are getting somewhere and in fact, your practice may well be showing signs of becoming deeper and more robust. The pitfall is when you inflate such experiences or thoughts and you start believing in them as special. It's when you get attached to your experience that the practice arrests, and your development along with it.

T R Y : Whenever you find yourself thinking you are getting somewhere or that you're not getting where you are supposed to be, it can be helpful to ask yourself things like: "Where am I supposed to get?"; "Who is supposed to get somewhere?"; "Why are some mind states less valid to observe and accept as being present than others?"; "Am I inviting mindfulness into each moment, or indulging in mindless repetition of the forms of meditation practice, mistaking the form for the essence of it?"; "Am I using meditation as a technique?"

These questions can help you cut through those moments when self-involved feeling states, mindless habits, and strong emotions dominate your practice. They can quickly bring you back to the freshness and beauty of each moment as it is. Perhaps you forgot or didn't quite grasp that meditation really is the one human activity in which you are not trying to get anywhere else but simply allowing yourself to be where and as you already are. This is a bitter medicine to swallow when you don't like what is happening or where you find yourself, but it is especially worth swallowing at such times.

Is Mindfulness Spiritual?

If you look up the word "spirit" in the dictionary, you will find that it comes from the Latin, *spirare*, meaning "to breathe." The inbreath is inspiration; the outbreath expiration. From these come all the associations of spirit with the breath of life, vital energy, consciousness, the soul, often framed as divine gifts bestowed upon us, and therefore an aspect of the holy, the numinous, the ineffable. In the deepest sense, the breath itself is the ultimate gift of spirit. But, as we have seen, the depth and range of its virtues can remain unknown to us as long as our attention is absorbed elsewhere. The work of mindfulness is waking up to vitality in every moment that we have. In wakefulness, everything inspires. Nothing is excluded from the domain of spirit.

As much as I can, I avoid using the word "spiritual" altogether. I find it neither useful nor necessary nor appropriate in my work at the hospital bringing mindfulness into the mainstream of medicine and health care, nor in other settings in which we work such as our multi-ethnic inner-city stress reduction clinic, prisons, schools, and with professional organizations and athletes. Nor do I find the word "spiritual" particularly congenial to the way I hold the sharpening and deepening of my own meditation practice.

This is not to deny that meditation can be thought of fundamentally as a "spiritual practice." It's just that I have a problem with the inaccurate, incomplete, and frequently misguided connotations of that word. Meditation can be a profound path for developing oneself, for refining one's perceptions, one's views, one's consciousness. But, to my mind, the vocabulary of spirituality creates more practical problems than it solves.

Some people refer to meditation as a "consciousness discipline." I prefer that formulation to the term "spiritual practice" because the word "spiritual" evokes such different connotations in different people. All these connotations are unavoidably entwined in belief systems and unconscious expectations that most of us are reluctant to examine and that can all too easily prevent us from developing or even from hearing that genuine growth is possible.

On occasion, people come up to me in the hospital and tell me that their time in the stress reduction clinic was the most spiritual experience they ever had. I am happy that they feel that way because it is coming directly out of their own experience with the meditation practice, and not from some theory or ideology or belief system. I usually think I know what they mean; but I also know that they are trying to put words to an inward experience which is ultimately beyond labels. But my deepest hope is that whatever their experience or insight was, it will continue for them, that it will take root, stay alive, grow.

Hopefully they will have heard that the practice is not about getting anywhere else at all, not even to pleasant or profound spiritual experiences. Hopefully they will come to understand that mindfulness is beyond all thinking, wishful and otherwise, that the here and now is the stage on which this work unfolds continuously.

The concept of spirituality can narrow our thinking rather than extend it. All too commonly, some things are thought of as spiritual while others are excluded. Is science spiritual? Is being a mother or father spiritual? Are dogs spiritual? Is the body spiritual? Is the mind spiritual? Is childbirth? Is eating? Is painting, or playing music, or taking a walk, or looking at a flower? Is breathing spiritual, or climbing a mountain? Obviously, it all depends on how you encounter it, how you hold it in awareness.

Mindfulness allows everything to shine with the luminosity that the word "spiritual" is meant to connote. Einstein spoke of "that cosmic religious feeling" he experienced contemplating the underlying order of the physical universe. The great geneticist Barbara McClintock, whose research was both ignored and disdained by her male colleagues for so many years until it was finally recognized at age eighty with a Nobel Prize, spoke of "a feeling for the organism" in her efforts to unravel and understand the intricacies of corn genetics. Perhaps ultimately, spiritual simply means experiencing wholeness and interconnectedness directly, a seeing that individuality and the totality are interwoven, that nothing is separate or extraneous. If you see in this way, then everything becomes spiritual in its deepest sense. Doing science is spiritual. So is washing the dishes. It is the inner experience which counts. And you have to be there for it. All else is mere thinking.

At the same time, you have to be on the lookout for tendencies toward self-deception, deluded thinking, grandiosity, self-inflation, and impulses toward exploitation and cruelty directed at other beings. A lot of harm has come in all eras from people attached to one view of spiritual "truth." And a lot more has come from people who hide behind the cloak of spirituality and are willing to harm others to feed their own appetites.

Moreover, our ideas of spirituality frequently ring with a slightly holier-than-thou resonance to the attuned ear. Narrow, literalist views of spirit often place it above the "gross," "polluted," "deluded" domain of body, mind, and matter. Falling into such views, people can use ideas of spirit to run from life.

From a mythological perspective, the notion of spirit has an upwardly rising quality, as James Hillman and other proponents of archetypal psychology point out. Its energy embodies ascent, a rising above the earthbound qualities of this world to a world of the non-material, filled with light and radiance, a world beyond opposites, where everything merges into one-ness, nirvana, heaven, a cosmic unity. But, while unity is surely an all-too-rare human experience, it is not the end of the story. What is more, all too often it is merely nine parts wishful thinking (but thinking nonetheless) and only one part direct experience. The quest for spiritual unity, especially in youth, is often driven by naivete and a romantic yearning to transcend the pain, the suffering, and the responsibilities of this world of eachness and suchness, which includes the moist and the dark.

The *idea* of transcendence can be a great escape, a high-octane fuel for delusion. This is why the Buddhist tradition, especially Zen, emphasizes coming full circle, back to the ordinary and the everyday, what they call "being free and easy in the market-place." This means being grounded *anywhere*, in any circum-stances, neither above nor below, simply present, but *fully* pres-ent. And Zen practitioners have the wholly irreverent and wonderfully provocative saying, "If you meet the Buddha, kill him," which means that any conceptual attachments to Buddha or enlightenment are far from the mark.

Notice that the mountain image as we use it in the moun-tain meditation is not merely the loftiness of the peak, high above all the "baseness" of quotidian living. It is also the groundedness of the base, rooted in rock, a willingness to sit and be with all conditions, such as fog, rain, snow, and cold or, in terms of the mind, depression, angst, confusion, pain, and suffering.

Rock, the students of psyche remind us, is symbolical of *soul* rather than *spirit*. Its direction is downward, the soul journey a symbolic descent, a going underground. Water, too, is symbolical of soul, embodying the downward element, as in the lake meditation, pooling in the low places, cradled in rock, dark and mysterious, receptive, often cold and damp.

The soul feeling is rooted in multiplicity rather than oneness, grounded in complexity and ambiguity, eachness and suchness. Soul stories are stories of the quest, of risking one's life, of enduring darkness and encountering shadows, of being buried underground or underwater, of being lost and at times confused, but persevering nevertheless. In persevering, we ultimately come in touch with our own goldenness as we emerge from the darkness and the submerged gloom of the underground that we most feared but nevertheless faced. This goldenness was always there, but it had to be discovered anew through this descent into darkness and grief. It is ours even if it remains unseen by others or even at times by us ourselves.

Fairy tales in all cultures are for the most part soul stories rather than spirit stories. The dwarf is a soul figure, as we saw in "The Water of Life." Cinderella is a soul story. The archetype there is ashes, as Robert Bly pointed out in *Iron John*. You (because these stories are all about you) are kept *down*, in the ashes, close to the hearth, grounded but also grieving, your inner beauty unperceived and exploited. During this time, inwardly, a new development is taking place, a maturation, a metamorphosis, a tempering, which culminates in the emergence of a fully developed human being, radiant and golden, but also wise to the ways of the world, no longer a passive and naive agent. The fully developed human being embodies the unity of soul and spirit, up and down, material and non-material.

The meditation practice itself is a mirror of this journey of growth and development. It too takes us down as well as up, demands that we face, even embrace, pain and darkness as well as joy and light. It reminds us to use whatever comes up and wherever we find ourselves as occasions for inquiry, for opening, for growing in strength and wisdom, and for walking our own path.

For me, words like "soul" and "spirit" are attempts to describe the inner experience of human beings as we seek to know ourselves and find our place in this strange world. No truly spiritual work could be lacking in soul, nor can any truly soulful work be devoid of spirit. Our demons, our dragons, our dwarfs, our witches and ogres, our princes and princesses, our kings and queens, our crevices and grails, our dungeons and our oars are all here now, ready to teach us. But we have to listen and take them on in the spirit of the heroic never-ending quest each of us embodies, whether we know it or not, in the very fabric of a human life lived, for what it means to be fully human. Perhaps the most "spiritual" thing any of us can do is simply to look through our own eyes, see with eyes of wholeness, and act with integrity and kindness.

✣

. . . their eyes, their ancient glittering eyes, are gay.

W . B . YEATS, *Lapiz Lazuli*

Afterword

I don't imagine people buy books about meditation all that casually. The fact that this one has now been in print for ten years and is in over twenty languages suggests that people are being drawn to and touched by its basic message, perhaps because we are so starved for our own direct experience of being who we somehow know deep down we already are, but perhaps feel slightly at a distance from all the same. Perhaps it is tapping an increasingly widespread and deep yearning for authenticity, intimacy, and clarity, and reminding us of what we already know: that these qualities can be found only within ourselves and within the unfolding of our direct experience of living, and that that unfolding is always and only here, and always and only now, whatever our circumstances. Perhaps people recognize in the title the calling to wake up to our experience while we have the chance, and how easy it is to sleepwalk through and therefore miss much of our life, telling ourselves nice stories of who we are and where we are going, along the way to some deluded fantasy we may never reach and might never recover from were we to arrive.

This book is so close to my heart, and it feels so complete to me as it is, that, when asked to write something for this tenth anniversary edition, I found myself reluctant to introduce new material at the beginning, in the form of a foreword. Hence, this Afterword.

There is much to say, and, at the same time, nothing to say. The meditation practice itself is timeless, and it is deeply gratifying to see it taking root so deeply in our society at a time of such great inner and outer turmoil and confusion, and at a time of such ferocious time-acceleration, driven by the advent of the digital age and feeding our capacity for getting more and more done in less and less time, thereby dramatically increasing the risk of never being present with and for ourselves, of losing touch almost entirely with the domain of being. Nothing like this has ever been seen in the entire trajectory of humanity. The species itself is at a critical juncture, a tipping point, and mindfulness, our innate capacity for wakefulness and open-hearted presence and clear seeing, has never been more critically important.

To my mind, what we need, now more than ever, within all the turmoil, is an inner wisdom, a rotation in consciousness, to accompany and shape the trajectory of our various engagements in the world, as well as to guide us individually and collectively in the full development of our potential as human beings. Mindfulness meditation, especially when it is understood as a way of being, as living life as if it really mattered, moment by moment by moment, rather than merely as a technique or as one more thing you have to do during your already too-busy day, is one powerful vehicle for realizing such transformative and healing possibilities in ourselves and in the world. And because it is a door into the timeless, it operates beyond time, underneath time, inside of time, and so allows for transformation without having to strive to get anywhere else, or beat oneself up along the way for being inadequate, or imperfect.

For, as the book affirms, you are already perfect. We all are. Perfectly what we are, including all our imperfections and inadequacies. The question is: can we be with it? Can we sit with it? Can we know it? Can we embrace our own wholeness and embody it, here, where we already are, in the very situations, good, bad, ugly, lost, confusing, heart-rending, terrifying, and painful, that we find ourselves in? Can we be this knowing? Can we realize the infinite beauty and mystery and intelligence of our own awareness and realize, too, that it can be infinitely refined through tending, through the cultivation of an affectionate and tender attention? Can we realize that wherever we go, there we are and that this "there" is always "here" and so requires at least acknowledgment and perhaps a degree of acceptance of what is, however it is, because it already is? Can we grow into ourselves in our fullness and live our precious and fleeting lives more wisely?

These are all one question really. And the gut response is, We can, we can.... When you come right down to it, what else is there to do? And what could be more important than to give our very life, in the fullness of its possibilities and its very actualities, often unseen, unnoticed, and unused, back to ourselves while we have the chance? It is either "Wherever you go, there you are," or "Wherever you go, there you aren't." Both are true to a degree in any moment. But we can fiddle with the degreeness, and so reclaim who and what we already are, and always have been, right here, right now ... only temporarily forgotten.

Mindfulness, cultivated for even a few minutes, draws the heart toward itself. It invites the intimacy we yearn for and that is calling to us because, ultimately, mindfulness is intimacy—with ourselves and the world—underneath any apparent separation between the two. The practice of mindfulness immediately makes available to us both the world's and our heart's intrinsic goodness and beauty, revealing through our direct experience the power and solace of resting in the present moment in awareness, out of the wind of our afflictive emotions and the agitations of an unquiet and continually judging mind, revealing as well that these cannot but abate on their own if we cease denying them or attempting to shut them down, which only feeds their disquieting energies and so often leads to harm and suffering in all directions, inwardly and outwardly, rather than to illumination and kindness.

The deepest of bows to you for the courage and perseverance involved in throwing yourself wholeheartedly into this adventure of a lifetime. In our everyday lives, we are all embodying and mirroring the myriad emergent forms of the possible for each other and for the world itself, moment by moment and breath by breath. With every breath, we are continually invited to embody and therefore actualize the possible more consistently, more ardently, more compassionately, with greater appreciation for the clarity, sanity, and well-being that are always and already right beneath our noses, and within all of us.

May we continue to give ourselves over to what is deepest and best in ourselves, over and over and over again, encouraging those seeds of our truest nature to grow and flower and—for the sake of all beings near and far, known and unknown—nourish our lives and work and world from moment to moment, and from day to day.

Jon Kabat-Zinn
Spring 2004

Mindfulness Meditation Practice CDs
With Jon Kabat-Zinn

There are three sets of Mindfulness Meditation Practice CDs.

They can be ordered directly from the website:
www.mindfulnesstapes.com

SERIES 1

(4 CDs) contains the guided meditations [the body scan and sitting meditation] and guided mindful yoga practices used by people who enrolled in Dr. Kabat-Zinn's classes in the Stress Reduction Clinic at the University of Massachusetts Medical Center. These practices are described in detail in *Full Catastrophe Living*. Each CD is 45 minutes in length.

SERIES 2

(4 CDs) is designed for people who want a range of shorter guided meditations to help them develop and/or expand a personal meditation practice based on mindfulness. The series includes the mountain and lake meditations (each 20 minutes) described in this book, as well as a range of other 10 minute, 20 minute, and 30 minute sitting and lying down practices. This series was originally developed to complement this book.

(4 CDs) is designed to accompany Dr. Kabat-Zinn's latest book, *Coming to Our Senses*. Programs include mindfulness of breath and body sensations; mindfulness of sounds and hearing; mindfulness of thoughts and feelings; cultivating choiceless awareness; and loving-kindness meditation. All programs are 20–30 minutes in length.

For more information, as well as to order, see:

www.mindfulnesstapes.com

Note: Series 1 and Series 2 are also available as audiocassette programs.

The author gratefully acknowledges permission from these sources to reprint the following:

From *I Am That; Talks with Sri Nisargadatta Maharaj*. Translated from the Marathi tape recordings by Maurice Frydman; edited by Sukhar S. Dikshit. Copyright 1973 Chetana Pvt. Ltd., Bombay. First American edition published by The Acorn Press, Durham, N.C., 1982, sixth printing 1992. Reprinted by permission of the American publisher.

Portions reprinted from *The Enlightened Heart* by Stephen Mitchell (Wu-men, Chuang Tzu, Li Po, Issa, Basso, Dogen), Harper & Row, 1989.

From *The Kabir Book* by Robert Bly. Copyright © 1971, 1977 by Robert Bly. Reprinted by permission of Beacon Press.

Martha Graham quoted in article by Agnes DeMille published in *The New York Times*, Sunday, April 7, 1991.

Portions reprinted from *Tao Te Ching*, trans. by Stephen Mitchell, HarperPerennial, 1988.

Specified excerpt from *The Practice of the Wild* by Gary Snyder. Copyright © 1990 by Gary Snyder. Reprinted by permission of North Point Press, a division of Farrar, Straus & Giroux, Inc.

Selection reprinted from *The Joy of Insight* by Victor Weisskopf, Basic Books, 1991.

Excerpt from *The Snow Leopard* © 1978 by Peter Matthiessen used by permission of Viking Penguin a division of Penguin USA.

Selection reprinted from John Steinbeck and Edward Ricketts, *Sea of Cortez*, 1941. Used by permission of Appel Publishers.

Selection reprinted from *Wholeness and the Implicate Order* by David Bohm, 1980, Routledge & Kegan Paul, London, Boston. Used by permission of the publisher.

From *The World as I See It*, © 1956, 1984 by the Estate of Albert Einstein. Published by arrangement with Carol Publishing Group.

From the book *Introduction to Zen Buddhism* by D. T. Suzuki, copyright © 1964 by D. T. Suzuki. Used with the permission of Grove/Atlantic Monthly Press.

Selection reprinted with permission of Macmillan Publishing Company from *The Poems of W. B. Yeats: A New Edition*, edited by Richard J. Finneran. Copyright 1940 by Georgie Yeats, renewed 1968 by Bertha Georgia Yeats, Michael Butler Yeats, and Anne Yeats.

Quotations from Gandhi are reprinted by kind permission of the Navajivan Trust, Ahmedabad 14, India.

The author also wishes to acknowledge the following reprinted material for

About the Author

Jon Kabat-Zinn, Ph.D., is a meditation teacher, scientist, and writer. He is Professor of Medicine emeritus at the University of Massachusetts Medical School, where he was founding executive director (in 1995) of the Center for Mindfulness in Medicine, Health Care, and Society, and founder (in 1979) and former director of its world-renowned Stress Reduction Clinic. His work was featured in the 1993 PBS Series, *Healing and the Mind, with Bill Moyers*. He is also the author of *Full Catastrophe Living: Using the Wisdom of Your Body and Mind to Face Stress, Pain and Illness* (Delta, 1991), *Coming to Our Senses: Healing Ourselves and the World Through Mindfulness* (Hyperion, 2005), and co-author, with his wife, Myla, of *Everyday Blessings: The Inner Work of Mindful Parenting* (Hyperion, 1997). He is Senior Advisor to the Consortium of Academic Health Centers for Integrative Medicine, and is on the Board of the Mind and Life Institute, a group that organizes dialogues between the Dalai Lama and Western scientists to promote deeper understanding of different ways of knowing and researching the nature of the mind, emotions, and reality. He has trained groups of judges, business leaders, lawyers, clergy, Olympic athletes (the 1984 Olympic Men's Rowing Team), and environmental activists in mindfulness. Under his direction, the Center for Mindfulness conducted mindfulness-based stress reduction (MBSR) programs in the inner city in Spanish as well as in English, and in the state prison system in Massachusetts. He conducts annual mindfulness retreats for business leaders and innovators, and with his colleagues in the Center for Mindfulness, leads training retreats for health professionals in MBSR. His work and that of his colleagues at UMass and around the world has contributed to a growing movement of mindfulness into mainstream institutions in our society such as medicine, health care and hospitals, schools, corporations, prisons, and professional sports.

The mountain just sits, while everything else changes around it; it simply remains itself (232)